THE STORM

BY RICKY G. STANLEY

Author of "Pretty Ricky Goes To Jail"

Edited by Ricky G. Stanley

rickystanley425@gmail.com

Copyright © 2016 Ricky G. Stanley All rights reserved.

No part of this book may be reproduced, stored for retrieval or transmission by any source without written permission of the author.

ISBN: 1536949116
ISBN 13: 978-1536949117

All persons characterized in this work are imaginary and are used to support the fictional subject matter. Any scenario which might appear to be similar to any real-life situations are merely coincidental.

Acknowledgement

First acknowledging my Lord and Savior, Jesus Christ; without Whom this nor I would exist. Thank You for saving me from myself. Secondly, this book is dedicated to my family who has been my inspiration, my encouragement, and my reason for continuing to strive to be the best version of myself. Finally, this book is to anyone who refuses to put limits on dreamers. Thank you for inspiring us to climb higher!

Ricky

Preface

Hello, my name is Ricky G. Stanley. I have created a new series of inspirational books and in this one I have a wonderful story to tell you about a wonderful family who through life's trials and travesties found glory and the Light.

Meet The Johnsons

Deep in the woods lived the family of Tim and Emma Johnson. The Johnsons had nine children, three boys: Andrew, Alvin, and Kelvin and six girls: Sharon, Deborah, Barbara, Gabby, Marian, and Cindy. As you would imagine Tim and Emma struggled just to keep enough food on the supper table for their family. Tim was deployed in the United States Army where he served as a Drill Sargent stationed in Fort Stewart, Georgia. He chose to stay enlisted because of the extra income and benefits it allowed him and his family. Emma, a stay-at-home mom, was the primary responsible person for the children while Tim was away.

Every day they would sit down and the mother would stand up to bless the food. She would thank God for what they had and thank Him for what they did not have to go through. She was thankful. As she asked God to keep her family close together and to watch over them day and night. But, along with her prayer, she prayed a special prayer for her youngest son, Kelvin. Mothers always carried a special affection for their baby boys and Kelvin was no exception. The oldest son, Andrew, who was in high school, was about to graduate. It was scorching hot outside that late June summer day as the mailman came by bringing a certified letter for Mrs. Emma Johnson that was marked "urgent." The look on his face told her he had delivered more than this one and did not enjoy the trip. Emma immediately torn into the envelop and began to read. "To Mrs. Emma Johnson, we have tried to get in touch with you numerous times using the sheriff department, email, and by telephone. As a result, we are attempting to contact you by certified mail. Please contact me as soon as possible after you read this letter." Mrs. Johnson's hands trembled terribly as she frantically dialed the telephone number for the person who sent her the letter. "How may I help you?" the operator robotically announced into the phone. Mrs. Johnson's voice shook out the details of the letter she received and the operator quickly connected her to a military officer. Major Larry Bullock had the voice of a very soft spoken, consoling man. His voice was almost too soothing as he explained the reasons for the previous urgency in trying to reach Mrs. Johnson. "It is with the deepest regret that I must inform you of the untimely death of Drill Sargent Mr. Tim Johnson. Emma learned that her husband had been killed by a suicide bomber in Kuwait in the line of duty three days ago. We unwaveringly tried to use every available resource to find you." Emma sat stiff, frozen…completely paralyzed. "Mrs. Johnson? Are you okay?" The officer wanted to be sure she did not need him to call medical care for her. In her stupor, Emma had dropped the phone. She blankly stared ahead as she went outside to sat on the swing that Tim Johnson had built and hung on the shady side of the porch just for her. She sat there swing gently back and forth…just rocking away. Then the tears started to flow as if someone cut on the faucets within her mind. "Why, God?!" "What did I do to have this to happen to me?" "Why did you take my husband from me?" "How am I supposed to manage taking care of nine children all by myself?!" Emma just sat there with those thoughts screaming through her mind. What was she going to say to their children? When she shook free from her daze, she looked directly into the eyes of Andrew, her oldest son. He had been standing before her staring at her because he could plainly see that his mother had been crying. He asked her what had happened to make her cry. Emma told him she would talk to him and his sibling when everyone was gathered in the living room. She asked him to go get his siblings for her.

Once everyone had gathered in the living room, they all sat in total silence. Andrew had warned them that this was very important and they were to be on their best behavior. Emma began to recount the events of her day. When she came to the part about the letter, the children all sat wide-eyed in total disbelief. One by one they screamed and hugged each other as the news slowly resonated like a black cloud of smoke covering the hopes of everyone in the room. Emma's heart broke for them and with them. She did not feel like this was the appropriate time, but she felt she had to stress this meant she would be their only source of income and times would get really tight, so everyone had to do their part to help out to make the family stay strong and stay together. Each person was expected to carry their own weight. Andrew, being the oldest, would make decisions when Emma was unavailable and the younger siblings were to follow his instructions. This assignment of duties would not be easy on anyone so it was reiterated that all the children would have added responsibilities and would also be expected to support one another. The family's struggle became even more challenging as time went on, but each of the children graduated high school and began to start their own families.

Several years of highs and lows passed, but the family unit remained intact. It had been five years since the death of Tim Johnson when Emma called

Kelvin, her youngest son, into her bedroom. "Kelvin, you know the struggles I went through trying to feed nine children. Promise me you will not go out into the world and have a bunch of children unless you know for sure you can take care of them." Kelvin promised his mother he would do as she requested.

Kelvin

After his high school graduation, Kelvin began working on the automobile assembly line for a major auto maker. He would call his mother to tell her how much he loved his new job. Emma would remind him to be grateful and to always give thanks to God for giving him the job.

"Your God has always looked out for you, Kelvin," she said. She would remind him how important it was for him to attend Bible Class. Kelvin would tell her he found it hard to attend the classes due to his early morning schedule. Emma reminded her son to pray and to read his Bible even when he could not attend the classes. She wanted him to stay connected to the Lord because she understood how pride came before a fall and she did not want Kelvin's newfound wealth to lead him away from the God who had brought him out of poverty. Although he was a grown man, Emma still worried about her youngest son.

Kelvin meet a woman named Anna Gatlin. The very first time Kelvin saw her he knew in his heart she was the one for him. Kelvin begin dating Anna. They enjoyed attending church together on Sundays. When Kelvin asked Anna to marry him, she told him she would if he would marry her in the next two weeks. Kelvin didn't think anything was wrong with her requests so he broke the news to his mother. Emma was mortified, "Think about what you are saying, Kelvin!" "This is not a game!"

"This is your life!" Emma wanted Kelvin to understand that she respected the fact that he was a grown man and was very capable of making his own decisions, but she wanted him to think hard on this decision. She asked him to take his time and not be rushed into a situation that could be easy to get into, but very hard to come away from. She wanted him to be reassured that she would honor his decision, but as his mother it was her responsibility to advise him to be prudent in his decision making on a matter as important as this one.

Kelvin assured his mother that from the very first time he met Anna he was sure she would be his wife. He told his mother how much he loved her and why he loved her. Emma relented and accepted his decision. Two weeks after their conversation, Anna and Kelvin were married at the Johnson family church. His brothers served as his groomsmen. The wedding was packed with people from everywhere. All of Kelvin's sisters, their spouses, and children attended. It was a joyous occasion. Everything was beautiful. Kelvin was a happy man.

Within six months after the wedding, Kelvin became a deacon at his church. Kelvin found that his upbringing in the church served him well. He rekindled his relationship with God and was very grateful for all the things God had given him in the form of his wife and his job. He became the voice of the goodness of God. Kelvin was very engaged in the activities of the church and had strong a impact on the youth and the adults. The church membership began to grow. Kelvin would lead Bible Class discussions that were both relevant and practical. Everyone could feel Kelvin's anointing. Kelvin's pastor adored him and quickly begin grooming him for taking over the church in the pastor's absence. A year later, Kelvin became the pastor of the church after the pastor's untimely long term illness. Not long after he became the pastor, Kelvin and Anna announced they would become parents. Emma was thrilled with the direction Kelvin's life had taken. She constantly prayed for all of her children, and she especially thanked God for the things He was doing in Kelvin and Anna's lives. Emma could hardly wait until she was holding Kelvin's first baby. Everyone at the church was so excited for Anna and Kelvin. Emma was excited, but she also worried that Kelvin was putting too much on his plate with the job, the church and now a new baby. She prayed Kelvin would make sure he continued to be just as active in his marriage and in the baby's life as he was in the church. She had seen how having too much on one's plate always put the family last and she did not want what happened in her own marriage to happen to her son and Anna. Kelvin became a rising star among up and coming ministers in town. He was well spoken and his sermons made him one of the most sought after speakers in town. He was making quite a name for himself. Four years after the birth of their first child, Kelvin and Anna gave birth to their second baby. Now with two beautiful children, a growing ministry, the support of an entire community and the love they shared for each other, Kelvin and Anna had everything they desired in life.

Life Changes

Emma became very sick. She started to murmur to herself and would wonder off whenever given the opportunity. The doctors diagnosed her as having Alzheimer's. The disease was aggressively progressing Emma lost track of her own children's names very quickly. The Johnson children held a family meeting to discuss what should be done about their mother. It was decided that Andrew would hold the power of attorney for her financial and health care decisions. Everyone also agreed that she would be placed in an assisted living facility that specialized in treatment for Alzheimer patients as soon as it was reasonably possible. The one they chose was very near the automaker's plant where Kelvin worked so he agreed to visit her every day after work.

One of the nights while Kelvin sat in the chair visiting with his mother in hopes of helping her to remember who he was, she stared outside at something so distant it made Kelvin cry. He had dozed off when he first came to see her and had awaken wanting to talk with her. "Momma, if you can hear me, I know your mind is a thousand miles away, but I want to you know I will always love you." A huge lump logged in this throat as he said, "I will never miss a day coming to see you." Kelvin got up and left the room hurriedly. The ache in his heart bled to his soul. He had to get out of there! "Do you remember the promise you made to me?" Emma asked. Kelvin stopped dead in his tracks. He turned to look at her, still not believing what he thought he heard. She was looking at him from eyes that almost looked like his, waiting for his response. He ran over to her bed and grabbed her. "Yes, ma'am! I still remember exactly what I promised you, Momma." He cried into her shoulder. When he let go of her for fear he would break her, she had returned to her gaze out the window.

His mind raced to justify if what he thought had just happened was his imagination or his reality. In any case, he was glad for those few seconds he shared a moment with the woman he loved more than life. Kelvin gathered himself, told her how much he loved her and kissed her on the forehead. He eased her back under the covers and left for the evening.

Once he entered his house, he was emotionally spent. He plopped down in his favorite living room chair to recount what had just happened and quickly fell asleep. The next morning, it was Anna who after hearing his alarm clock went looking for him and found him fast asleep in the living room. "Did you sleep there all night?" she asked.

"Honey, it's time for you to go to work." He rose from his sleep and could not believe how exhausted he had been. He apologized to Anna for sleeping in the chair and made a vow to himself tell her about the last evening's occurrences at another time.

Anna fixed his usual breakfast and asked him what time did he get in. "Oh, about an hour ago," Kelvin said. "I went to visit my momma. She actually talked to me!" "That's good. I know you love your mother, but the rest of your family should go and sit with her, as well, you know." Anna stated. "I cannot speak for my siblings; I just do what I can for Momma the way I'm supposed to do." Kelvin said. He was still sleepy and knew today's lunchtime would be spent getting an hour of sleep. At work when the whistle rung to go back to work, Kelvin's boss came up to him on the assembly line and asked him to gather his gear and come to the office.

Once Kelvin was in the office, his was informed that he had to report home immediately. There had been an emergency. Kelvin asked what had happened and they stated they did not have any details; they received a request to ask him to return him as soon as possible. Anxiously, Kelvin clocked out with all types of worries dancing through his mind. He arrived home to see Anna pacing on the porch, awaiting his arrival. He ran up to her, "Anna, what's wrong?" "Momma Emma passed this morning around noon," she said.

Kelvin's entire world collapsed. Time completely stopped. He heard the rapid pulsation of his heartbeat in his ears and felt the pounding in the top of his head. This cannot be happening! He could not believe his mother was gone. Kelvin went to the room where he last saw his mother. His family was present in every bit of available space. He thought of the irony of seeing every one of them there now that she had died when not one of them thought to visit her while she lived. Alvin, the fourth child, said what everyone else must have been thinking, "Did Momma leave a will?" Kelvin looked at him with total disgust. "Is that all you can think about, right now? A will?" Kelvin asked him, but really was asking them all. He could not believe the only thing that could force them to visit their mother was to see if she left them anything. The answer, of course, is "No!"

"Not one red cent!" Kelvin smirked silently, "She left everything in my name and I'm not telling them anything.

Let them find out on their own." They probably didn't even have the decency to contact Andrew even though he was the executor of their mother's estate.

Kelvin called Andrew informing him of their mother's death. Andrew stated he would join them on the following evening. Kelvin told Andrew about Alvin's question. "Don't let that bother you, man, just hang in there until tomorrow and we will get things settled." Andrew said. Andrew arrived as planned the next day. There was a family meeting to discuss how they were to bury their mother. Kelvin said, "Our mother had an insurance policy for $150,000 that had me as the beneficiary." Alvin quickly chimed in, "How did you know that?" To which Kelvin stated, "If you came to visit her more often you would know that she left everything to me. Alvin was in a huff!

"You know momma was out of her mind when she left everything to you!" "You need to share with everyone else!" "Stop it, Alvin!" Andrew shouted! "Look at you!

You come here high on drugs and you think someone's going to give you a dime so you can get even higher! Our mother worked her fingers to the bone for us! You will not disrespect her last earnings with your bad behavior! Leave it alone!" Alvin looked at Andrew in total discontent, "Look at you! You come back home in your decked out Marine uniform on acting like you some big shot! I didn't see you here waiting on momma either! You were out somewhere playing Rambo for the military when your mother needed you!"

Alvin rose from his seat. "I'm not going to sit here and argue with you because you are absolutely pathetic. "You are on cloud nine, so I'd advise you to take your raggedy tail and get out of my face!" "Or, what?!" Alvin replied. "You'll kill me like you've been killing them innocent people overseas?" Andrew looked at Alvin and "You're not worth it!" Andrew turned and walked away.

Alvin smiled and said, "You're still the same coward you always were. And, you have the nerve to be wearing a Marine outfit." Kelvin stood between them and grabbed Andrew by the shoulders and ushered him outside the room. It was best they separated from one another until after the funeral. The priority now was to bury their mother and that had to come before everything else.

Ms. Emma

All of Emma's old neighborhood friends, the church family, and the people from where she had worked…almost the entire community showed up to say their goodbyes to Emma. The fact that so many people filled the church spoke to the kind of life Emma lived. Rev. Jasper preached her funeral! He told how she was always inviting one more person to sit at the table with her and her nine children. He spoke of how she taught her children to help in the community and how she taught them all to finish school. Yes, Emma's funeral was a hallelujah good time. The choir sung until Heaven got happy!

Emma grew up in Ahoskie, North Carolina, which was the largest community in Hertford County. This little township is located in the northeastern part of North Carolina on the Pleasure Route, US Highway 13, and is 24 miles south of the Virginia line. Emma's family moved there before the electrical lines were installed. Her parents had four daughters and she was the youngest of them. Her parents were farmers. Without boys in the family, Emma was the one who learned how to make the Earth fertile and how to make it grow whatever she planted. She would show her sons how to use this talent to grow huge gardens of their own.

Emma had always been a giver and believed in the importance of creating a community of givers. This would be an attribute she would demonstrate before her children. No one had to ask her if she would contribute to a needy family. Normally, even as a child, she was the first one to pitch in to walk their children to the one room school house or baby sit the children while the parents went to look for work. Emma was loved by everyone she met and it was evident by all those who showed up on this day to show their respect to the lady who not only told them how to love, but showed them how to love because she loved them when they felt unlovable.

When Emma married Tim, they agreed that her first job would be their six children. Tim was the ultimate provider. His family came first. He reenlisted to get the bonus in hopes of taking some of the pressure of their tight financial situation. Although sometimes it seemed like there was barely enough to go around, Emma had always been able to stretch whatever Tim provided to feed their family and any transits that happen to spend a few days or months at their home. She would always make room for one more.

Andrew

As they put the last dirt over Emma's casket, her children embraced each other. All nine of them were together. That is what Emma fought the hardest to maintain. She wanted her children to love each other no matter what happened. As Kelvin hugged Alvin, he noticed Alvin smelled of marijuana. "Man, you couldn't leave those drugs alone for one day to honor your own mother?" Kelvin asked him. "Get the Hell out of my face! Why don't you just go enjoy your $150,000." Alvin spat back at him. Kelvin turned and walked away from him.

On Sunday, Kelvin chose for his topic, "I've Been In The Storm Too Long." He had everyone on their feet shouting and praising God like no one had ever seen before at his church. After the service, the worshippers told Pastor Kelvin he was on fire! "You know, we all have our storms to go through, one day or another," Kelvin replied.

The word spread about this new fire that was burning in Kelvin since he had buried his mother. He was one of the most requested guest ministers in the city. His fame began to grow and he was reaching his peak. He felt like he was sitting at the top of the world He could begin to feel a shift in how he carried himself. It was like something strange had come over him. Something new was slowly taking hold of him. He was sitting in his study one afternoon feeling very strange and the phone ring. It wasn't just any ring; it was as if Kelvin had been expecting the phone to ring.

When he answered, he learned that his brother, Andrew, had been injured in the line of duty. "Are you sure you have the right Andrew Johnson?" Kelvin asked. The officer stated he was sure the person injured was his brother Andrew Johnson. At which point, Kelvin asked well how was he? The commanding officer stated that at Andrew's request the Marines were not to inform the family of his injury unless Andrew did not make it, and that Andrew had passed earlier that afternoon. Kelvin was speechless.

It felt like it had been forever, but Kelvin knew he would have to share the news with his siblings. He was spellbound, so much so that Anna walked over to him. "Is everything ok?" she asked. Kelvin did not know how to respond. The words would not form in his mind to come out of his mouth. He just looked up at her with such a painful stare that she flinched. Again, she asked, "Is everything ok, Kelvin?" Slowly, his brain began to function again and he whispered just loud enough for her to barely hear, "Andrew is dead." She jumped back, thinking she did not hear him correctly. "What did you say?" she asked leaning in closer. "Are you sure?" "How could that be true?" Kelvin explained the phone call and reached for his phone to begin calling his siblings to meet at the family house.

The family house was where all important decisions were made. It was also where all bad news was shared. Kelvin got there first so that he could receive his brother, his sisters and their spouses. As he explained the phone call, it was Alvin who took it the worse. He remembered the last exchange he had with Andrew and guilt ate him up like yesterday's leftover barbecue. His sister Sharon embraced him, "Alvin, we all have said things we didn't mean. I know in your case you think you didn't get to apologize, but remember what Momma always told us, "Where there is life, there is hope." Ask God to forgive you and He will. Just repent for the argument you had with your brother." Alvin hugged his sister tight and cried like he hadn't cried in years. They prayed together and he vowed right then that if it took the rest of his life, he would make amends of what happened between Andrew and him. The family spent time recounting the good times they all spent with Andrew and how he ordered them around when he was placed in charge. They wanted to fondly remember their brother. As they laughed and cried, the afternoon slowly faded into evening and the evening had quietly turned into night. It was time for them all to leave. Kevin would keep them all informed once Andrews remains arrived. As Alvin left he gave Kelvin a huge hug and told him he was so sorry for all the mean, hurtful things he had said in the past. He told Kelvin about the time he spent praying with Sharon and how he felt like he was strong enough to make concrete changes in his life. Kelvin hugged him back and together they rejoiced for Alvin's transformation that was about to happen in a big way.

Saying Goodbye To Alvin

On the day of Andrew's funeral, Kelvin preached a sermon entitled, *"Come to Take My People Back"* for his brother's funeral. There was not a dry eye in the house as Kelvin got so emotional in talking about how Jesus was coming to get His people one at a time and on that Great Day, He would come for them all at once. As Kelvin's emotions got the better of him, a deacon helped him from the pulpit and instructed the choir to begin singing, "Soon and Very Soon."

The deacons opened the doors of the church. Alvin stood straight up as if something in his seat made him sprang to his feet. He stood completely still with his eyes closed rocking to the music. Then, he made his way to the front of the church where the deacons helped him to a seat. Alvin rededicated his life to Christ. After hearing Alvin's name over the PA system, Kelvin came from the back of the church and went straight to hug his older brother. "Welcome home, my brother," he said.

The funeral directors were called to the front of the church to give everyone instructions on how to proceed to the cemetery. The brothers and sisters all lined up in the beginning of the funeral procession to head to the National Cemetery in Chattanooga, Tennessee. Andrew would be buried with full military honors, including the twenty-one-gun salute and "Taps." The American flag that once covered Andrew's casket was neatly folded by the servicemen and given to Sharon, the oldest sister. Andrew's body would be laid to rest in the same section of the cemetery, but across from his mother and father. His sisters requested the releasing of the doves to symbolize that Alvin joined their parents in Heaven.

Later as the family had settled down at the family house, Kelvin went to Alvin, "You know you sure did slip one over on me tonight. I had no idea you were going to do that at Andrew's funeral." Alvin said, "I had to repent and ask God to forgive me for all the wrong I did to both of my brothers. Now I feel so much better about myself." Kelvin said, "Man, you just don't know how good I felt to see my older brother rededicating his life back to Jesus." Before they went their separate ways, they hugged one last time.

Alvin become very active in church. He even joined the male choir and began practicing to lead hymns. He would contribute to the discussions in Bible Study and attended church worship service every Sunday.

Kelvin's Turn

Andrew's death really hit Kelvin hard. He could not bring himself out of the deep depression he found himself spiraling in. Anna tried to be there for him, but he would just push her away. In his mind, she could not relate to how deep this pain in his soul ran. He had lost the only two people he loved more than life and he had no one else to confide in. Kelvin's withdrawal began to cause problems at home. On top of what he was experiencing, Anna started feeling very ill. She was always tired and as much as she wanted to help him come out of his deep depression, her own health began to demand her attention. She did not know what was wrong with her.

Kelvin tried to encourage her to go to the doctor, but she kept saying she didn't like to go to doctors unless she really had to go; they made her nervous. It was when Kelvin found her spitting up blood all over the toilet stool that he insisted that she go to the doctor that day. He said he would take her. He noticed she was looking very thin. Everything she ate came right back up. It took all of Anna's strength to get dressed and make it to the car. As they drove to the doctor's office, she looked at Kelvin's face. It was so stressed. She didn't want to add to what he was going through, but she felt like she was drowning and needed him to throw her a life line. "Baby...could you please take a few days off to help me with the kids? I've been so tired lately I feel like if I could get some rest, I could do better," she said. Kelvin continued to drive a little while longer in silence. Then, he instructed the car's phone to call his office. When his boss answered, he requested a week vacation. He explained he was on his way to the doctor with his wife and he needed to be with his family at this time. His boss wished him the best and advised him to let the office know if there was anything they could do to help him.

When they arrived at the hospital, the doctor quickly ordered blood tests and x-rays. They asked Kelvin to step outside the room while they prepped Anna for the tests. When he returned, she had wires and tubes running everywhere. He was shocked. "What's going on?" he asked the leading nurse. The nurse told Kelvin that the preliminary tests did show she has something going on and the doctor ordered fluids and an IV. By this time, Dr. Sessons walked into the room looking a bit concerned. "How long has she had these symptoms?" he asked Kelvin. Kelvin stated he really didn't know. He became aware of Anna's symptoms only recently. He explained to the doctor that he was in his own state of depression after losing his brother and he really had not noticed his wife having any great difficulties until recently.

Kelvin did remember about three months ago they both were awaken because she had bled profusely in the bed. Dr. Sessons asked why they did not come to emergency room or call him so they could have tests ran.

Kelvin repeated what his wife told him about doctors, to which Dr. Sessons shook his head. Dr. Sessons told Kelvin he would review the test results and see what the prognosis would be for Anna. He reminded Kelvin that whatever was happening had could possibly have had a three-month head start and he could not make any guarantees on what would happen. When Kelvin got to the lobby, Alvin stood up.

He was there with Kelvin and Anna's children. Kelvin asked him if he would watch them overnight. "I'm staying here with her to see what's going on," he stated. Alvin reassured his brother the children would be fine. He hugged Kelvin and took the children home with him. Dericka, the daughter and the oldest of the two children, asked, "Uncle Alvin, is Mommy going to die?" She was nine years old and Alvin knew the children were too young to be bother with what was happening around them. "Your mom is sick. She is in the hospital so they can give her a check-up," Alvin replied. "Then, will she come home tonight?" Dericka asked. Alvin didn't know how to answer the question without upsetting the child, so he replied, "She will come home as soon as the doctors provide her with a discharge paper for her release."

Alvin's wife, Gail welcomed the kids home. She took Kelvin's kids, cleaned them up, and put them to bed. When Gail came back out of the kids' bedroom and walked over to Alvin, she said to him, "I wasn't going to say anything while they were up, but why are Kelvin's kids here?" Alvin replied, "Those kids are my niece and nephew. My brother needed help, so I am helping." Gail snapped, "He didn't need our help when he was spending all of that money your mother left the family, now did he?" Alvin jumped up from his chair, pointing his finger at Gail,

"Now you listen here to me Gail, and listen good. That money was willed to him by our momma. I have already forgiven him for that. And, furthermore, that's the end of our discussion on that topic forever!" Gail looked at him with the utmost disgust. "Coward!" She threw over her shoulder as she left the room. Alvin yelled, "Satan get thee behind me!" in the direction she had just left. He thought that ended the discussion but as soon as he was able to calm himself, Gail came in the room in full stride, "I want those kids out of this house and I want them out of here right now!" she screamed. Alvin looked into Gail's eyes and thought he could clearly see the demons of Hell stirring in their midst.

Alvin stood up and looked her dead in the eyes. "Go ahead and act crazy if you want to Alvin! Those white folks will have your saved behind locked behind bars before you know where you were standing," she barked in his face. "Go ahead, slap me! You know you want too! You haven't changed. You are just fooling those church folks, but you haven't fooled me!" she raged. Alvin shifted to his left so he did not touch her and left the room. He walked back to the study, went over to his desk and fell to his knees to begin to pray.

Alvin was praying to God and he asking for strength. "Our Heavenly Father, I need You. God please help me to keep my temper," he pleaded. He began to tell God how hard it had been to maintain his promise since he rededicated his life to Jesus. He said it felt like everyone was constantly trying to push his buttons and make him go back to who he was before his rededication. "Lord, my wife Gail and I never had these types of problems, but since I committed to You, Lord, she has become selfish and so self-centered I do not recognize her. He did not want to cry, but the tears ran down his face like a faucet without a shut off value. He was so upset with Gail got up from his prayer to go back to deal with her; however, an angel of The Highest God. The angel stopped him and asked, "Alvin…where are you going?" In his rage, Alvin answered, "I'm going back in there and do what I should have done earlier…take care of my problem." The angel said, "Alvin, wait! God sent me to tell you He has heard your prayer tonight just like He heard your prayers when you were out in the world." Alvin froze. "Wait?" It was then that he realized he had been speaking to the angel. The angel continued, "God wants you to be patient. He will take care of it all. He will take care of all that troubles you. Every tribulation you are experiencing right now has purpose. You must see it through." Then, Alvin asked,

"What about Gail, my wife?" The angel replied, "It's already done. God knows exactly how much you can bear. Just stay on your knees praying to your God." Suddenly, the angel had disappeared, leaving Alvin feeling energized and restored. He felt rejuvenated.

When he walked back into the living room where his wife sat, he was humming, "Jesus, Keep Me Near The Cross," one of the old gospel hymns his mother sung to them as kids. Gail turned to look at him, but did not say a word. Alvin went to his bedroom and prepared for bed. As he stood under the hot water from the shower, he thanked God for sending the angel to comfort him.

He thanked Him for restoring his faith and for helping him to get back aligned with God's will for his life. Just as he finished his meditation, Gail brought him clean towels to dry himself. She very dryly said, "I don't know how I knew you needed these towels, but something told me to bring them to you, so here they are." Alvin smiled and said, "Thank you." After she walked out the door, Alvin looked toward Heaven and smiled. He dried off, put on his PJs and jumped under the covers.

The Return of Kelvin

The next day, Kelvin was lying on the couch in Anna's hospital room. Anna was still asleep. He got up, stood beside Anna's hospital bed, kneeled down, and begun to pray. Kelvin's prayer was for Anna's healing. He asked God to take away this unknown sickness that had the doctors baffled. The tests were inconclusive. Kelvin knew the Great Physician. He stayed on his knees praying and fasting for Anna's returned health for hours. When Dr. Sessons came into the hospital room the next morning, he tapped the shoulder of Kelvin who was lying on the couch to greet him with a good morning, but cringed when he saw how sunken and wild-eyed Kelvin's eyes appeared. He asked the nurse to quickly bring Kelvin some coffee and breakfast. He encouraged Kelvin to take care of him. He gave him the analogy of the crashing airplane. "You know, even in a falling airplane, the parent is asked to put their own oxygen mask on first before they can help their children." "You are no good to Anna if you are not well yourself, Mr. Johnson," Dr. Sessons cautioned him. He understood the power of prayer and understood Kelvin was a praying man, but his role as their family doctor was to advise him to keep his strength up because he had no idea what was attacking Anna's body nor did he know how long it would be before her condition would begin to reverse. He wanted to be sure Kelvin was prepared for the long haul. He left the room to see another patient and to allow Kelvin time to eat his breakfast and get himself together. Once he felt he had given him ample time to get himself together Dr. Sesson returned to Anna's room. He asked Kelvin to join him in the hallway so he could speak with him. As they both stood outside of Anna's door, he opened her chart and showed him the latest test results. Kelvin read the chart and his legs went numb. "Diagnosis: Colorectal Cancer: Stage 4=POSITIVE" it read. "What does that mean?" Kevin asked partially in vain. He knew exactly what it meant. He had seen that word so many times on the charts of his worshippers' family members. However, Anna never smoked cigarettes or drank alcohol. "Newer studies show that more people like Anna are getting cancer," Dr. Sesson stated. "Genetics, environments, chemicals, and diet can play a role in carcinogens as well," he stated. "No longer does the diagnosis of cancer depend on just one specific thing. I'm so sorry this is happening to Anna and you. It has progressed so fast; she's already in Stage 4, which is the final phase of this dreaded disease," he continued. "How long…?" The words had to be force out of Kelvin's throat. "No one can say with extreme certainty, but I estimate she has about 48-60 days, based on the last round of tests," the doctor said. Kelvin grabbed the doctor and sobbed uncontrollably. Dr. Sesson took him to a room on the other side of the hospital and allowed him to get the initial shock out of his system. Then he began to tell him his treatment plan. He would not begin a round of chemotherapy because the cancer was too far advanced. He would order a morphine drip to keep her comfortable and he wanted Kelvin to be present when he had the discussion with her, but Kelvin asked him to give him a few days to digest the news so that he would not break down in front of Anna. He wanted to be strong for her and it was too painful for him to do it that day. The doctor agreed to order the pump and give Kelvin a couple of days to get himself together before he broke the news to Anna. He would also advise all medical staff they were not to discuss her diagnosis with her.

Kelvin when back into the room with Anna. He noticed she was awake staring at the wall. "Baby, how are you feeling this morning?" "I'm a little weak. My stomach feels so full and sore," she said. It took everything within Kelvin to turn quickly so she did not see the tear that voluntarily ran down the side of his face. He tried to hide it, but she saw that he was crying. "What's wrong with you, Kelvin?" she asked. "You know, you have not been yourself since Alvin's death and I'm so sorry to be so sick, but I've been meaning to talk to you. Are you ok? Tell me what's going on with you!" He didn't know what to say.

She's lying in bed dying of cancer and she's worried about him and his problems. She reached out for his hand and held it. "I've been up for a couple of minutes and I kind of heard parts of the conversation between Dr. Sesson and you. I don't want to leave you and the kids. I want to live and grow old with you. I want to see our grandchildren." She started to cry. "I don't understand what it is I did that was so bad that this had to happen to me, Kelvin." Kelvin was speechless. He hated that she had heard the conversation and had been in the room to process the news all alone. "So how long do I have?", Anna asked. Kelvin stated in slightly more than a whisper, "48-60 days." "Only 48-60 days? That's all the time I have left?! "Yes, that's what the doctor said, but we can get a second opinion from another doctor."

Just then Dr. Sesson came back into the room. "She knows," Kelvin announced. Dr. Sesson's eyes widened. "She does?" Kelvin explained that she heard them and what he had told her. Kelvin explained that he would like to take her to another facility to get a second opinion, to which Dr. Sesson said he would do a referral to a doctor in another network. He had his nurse to arrange the appointment for Anna. Anna was discharged out of the hospital with instructions to be on bed rest until her appointment with the other doctor. She was given high doses of prescription pain medication to help her rest. Once she was home, Kelvin helped her into the house, ran her bath and helped her to relax while he called Alvin to bring the children home.

Just as he got Anna settled in the bed and fed, he could hear Alvin's car pull into the driveway. The children burst through the front door, which was never locked and came running up the stairs to see their parents, screaming their names. Kelvin stood at the top of the stairs to slow them down and gave them the biggest bear hug. He missed seeing them. "Where's Mommy?", they asked in unison.

"She is resting, which is what the doctor told her to do." Give her a minute to get herself together and I will let you two come in for just a moment. Remember, she's been very sick so don't jump on the bed and try not to be too noisy," Kelvin instructed them. "Where are my babies?" Anna yelled as she stood in the bedroom door in her robe. Lil' Kelvin and Dericka went running to hug her. "Be careful, kids!", Kelvin shouted. "Oh, they are alright," Anna said back to him. "I've really missed you two," Anna told them between hugs and kisses.

"Are you all hungry?" Anna asked them. "Uncle Alvin took us to breakfast this morning and we had bacon, eggs and pancakes!" Dericka replied. "Yes, they were so good, too!" Lil' Kelvin chimed in. Anna asked them if they had thanked him for being so nice to them. They both nodded. "Baby, are you strong enough to go to the park with the kids and me?" Kelvin asked Anna. "I was thinking it would be good if we spent our first day back together in the sunshine."

Anna begin to wrap her sweater around her frail body as she walked to the store. Her rapid weight loss was becoming more obvious every time Kelvin looked at her. His heart began to sink, but he knew he would need to be the strength for his family and he was determined he would be the man he had been taught by his mother to be for them. Lil' Kelvin and Dericka chanted in unison, "Mommy's going…Mommy's going…Mommy's going!"

When they arrived at the park, the kids raced to the swings, "I'm going to get it first," they screamed. Anna grabbed Kelvin's hand and started to cry. "I don't want to leave my kids," she murmured. Kelvin tried to be strong for the both of them, but his eyes begin to water, as well. "Baby, I don't want you to ever leave my side. I don't know what I will do with myself if you ever left me, Anna. Truth be told, I wish I could take your place. You know. Let you live and take care of our family. You are the one who has held us all together," Kelvin said. "I would never leave you all if I had any choice of it. I will always be watching over you," said Anna.

Having recomposed himself, Kelvin said, "Ok, enough of this sad talk. Let's enjoy your living while you are here. Baby, where shall we vacation this year?" "Boy, with all the medical expenses we are going to have related to my illness, you know we cannot go on a vacation wasting money traveling around the world this year," Anna said, halfway teasing. "Baby, I want to have fun, I just work all the time. And, if I'm not at work, I'm preaching or working in the church. So, let's just take some money out of the bank and travel to anywhere you want to go. It's not about traveling around the world. We will be making memories. I want whatever time we have together to be full of happiness." "Kelvin, I am happy. Just being here with you and the kids makes me happy. You have always been a wonderful husband to me. I have lived long enough to enjoy every moment we have spent together. I have enjoyed every moment of being with you, Kelvin." Anna said softly. "You know one of our goals is to send the kids off to college one day. That would make me happier than some vacation." Kelvin was humbled by her words. "Let's go play with the kids" he said to take the pressure off.

Anna and Kelvin held hands like new lovers and went to play with their children. "Push me Mommy" "No, push me first." The children yelled at their mother. Kelvin sat her on the park bench and went to push the children in the swings. That day would be the last good day they spent in their happy place, or so it would seem to Kelvin. The clock ticked much too fast for Anna, Kelvin thought as he sat next to her while she laid resting in their bed. She appeared to be losing her mind. The cancer had spread throughout her frail body until he barely recognized the human who laid there. It has been days since she had said anything. And, her last words were about some mystic unicorn who sprinkled the children with magical dust that made them real. Kelvin had no idea what that meant or where she may have gotten that idea from. What he did realize is that her time on Earth was drawing neigh and the Anna he had known and loved left days ago. This person she had become was lingering, but only for a little while longer. Even though she was a different Anna, he loved her just the same. He had been keeping his brother, Alvin updated on her progressive decline. It was Alvin he leaned on now that Andrew was deceased. Kelvin sat beside Anna, holding her hand. He started to hum "Precious Lord," a gospels song his mother song to him when she was troubled. When he finished the stanza, Anna's eyes seemed to relax as if he had given her permission to take her rest. That was the day she left him to join Tim, Emma and Andrew. His Anna had gone home to Glory.

Kelvin had prearranged Anna's burial plans so he called her doctor and mortician to announce her death. After he handle the formalities, he went to their bedroom and got on his knees and prayed. "Dear Father in Heaven, what am I supposed to do now. You have taken away my everything. You know I cannot function well without her. Lord, why would you give me the apple of my eye if this is how much pain you would cause me to have because of her? Why did you take her back and leave me with two minor children with no mother to help me raise them? Lord, I am so weak. My heart is hurting. What am I supposed to do by myself?" He just stayed there sobbing uncontrollably and feeling completely helpless.

When nighttime came, Kelvin tried his best to fall asleep, but his mind would not be quiet! He tossed and turned all night long. The next day, he received a phone call from Alvin. Kelvin attempted to put into words what it was like to lose the biggest part of himself. He felt completely lost without Anna. He wished God had taken him along with her he told Alvin. Alvin was new to this comforting role, but he knew he had to help his brother go through this grieving process. He always admired Kelvin and Anna's relationship. A part of him wanted that same type of relationship with Gail. He wanted to help his brother to see through the current pain so that he could come out of this lesson of learning whole. "I know you may not want to hear it right now, my brother, but God has a true reason for everything He does," Alvin told Kelvin. Kelvin's broken voice almost screamed back, "How can you say that when all I want to do is die, man?"

Alvin knew it would take time for Kelvin to come to his senses, "Man, look, you need to stop talking foolish. What would happen to Dericka and Lil' Kelvin if God took their mother and you?" The mere thought of that happening made Kelvin sick to his stomach. Alvin could hear him drop the phone and run to the bathroom, so he disconnected the call.

Each night Kelvin got into bed with Anna's presence on his mind. It was time to make sure things were in order for the funeral. Kelvin had delayed it as much as he could. Alvin came to take him to the funeral home after they had made the arrangements earlier. This would be the final private viewing before the public would be allowed to see her. Secretly, Alvin had already come by earlier to make sure things were in order because he did not want any added pressure to fall upon his brother during this difficult time.

As they walked into the chapel where the wake would be held, Alvin was telling Kelvin how beautiful Anna looked. Kelvin could barely see her through the tears that filled his eyes. He reached to grab her cold, hard hand. And he just stood there in a daze. She was the first woman he had ever loved and he loved her from the first time he saw her. "I don't want to live without her," he whispered to no one. Alvin overheard him and said, "Come on, man! You have got to be strong. You cannot allow your emotions to get the best of you now. I know you are hurting and while I don't know how much or what it feels like, I know the children are going to be hurting too. You are going to be who they look to for help to get through this."

As irrelevant as it may have sound, Kelvin said, "I don't even know how to pay bills, Alvin. She took care of all of that. I just made the money and she took care of the bills, the house and the children. When I say I am lost, I am truly lost, brother!" Alvin almost chuckled when he replied, "Well, you had better start learning and you better start learning fast because now, you are going to be doing all of that! It isn't as hard as you think and I can show you what I know." He could not believe that his brother, who appeared to have it all together did not know how to pay bills.

As it became time for their sisters and their families to join them at the funeral home, Kelvin, Alvin and Gail stood along with the kids to greet them. Gail made sure the children were properly dress to attend the funeral.

She had softened tremendously since that night when Anna went to the hospital. Alvin had watch God stay true to His promise. Gail had become a good auntie for the children. She voluntarily took them for ice cream and to play in the park to give Kelvin a break. The immediate family spent time alone before the church family and friends would join them. The children were embraced by their cousins. They were kept busy playing so they would not have time to spend crying for their mother.

The wake was held an hour before the funeral. Kelvin could not bear to prolong the services. When the funeral time came, the Minister Paul M. Nichols of the New United First Presbyterian Baptist Church stood up acknowledging how many people were in attendance. "This young woman must have been very caring to so many people. But, you know, it should not take a funeral to bring us together to recognize those who mean a great deal to us.

Death should never be the only reason we come to the House of God. And yet, we are here for the homegoing services of Mrs. Anna M. Johnson. Sister Anna came from a family of strong believers. When I say strong, I mean strong in the sense of she was loving and caring. Just like her family, Sister Anna cared for everyone who crossed her path that needed her. God gave her a special gift. I have seen times when the homeless would come to the church for food and shelter. Sister Anna would come out of her pocket with money to help provide for them, if the church did not have enough money. She was indeed a sweet lady. She has left behind a loving and kind family. Pastor Kelvin Johnson, her devoted husband is the example of husband's everywhere. He doted on her. Young men, if you ever want to know how God tells the man to love his wife, Minister Johnson is the example. Their children, Dericka and Lil' Kelvin are also known givers. These kids are at every food drive helping to load baskets and asking for donations. This is a special family." Elder Nichols went on to preach a sermon about "Your Life Is Your Eulogy."

He used how Anna had lived to teach others how what they do now will be what they are remembered by on the day of their funeral. Kelvin had requested one final viewing of Anna before they exited the church so the children could say their goodbyes. Dericka cried while touching her mother's face and asking her to wake up. "Why is Mommy still asleep? Why won't she wake up?" she asked.

The scene broke Kelvin's heart all over again. He quietly took the children out of the sanctuary to explain to them again that the body out there was the shell Mommy lived in. Mommy had left and is now in Heaven. Demandingly Lil' Kevin said, "Well, let's just go to Heaven and see her!" Alvin walked in to check on them. He allowed Kelvin to go back to say goodbye to his wife before the finally closed the casket. "I love you, Baby. Rest in peace," Kelvin said to her before the morticians sealed the casket. Alvin came from the back with the children so they could all get in the car for the ride to the cemetery. As the final rites were given and Anna's body was lowered into her grave, Alvin walked over to where Kelvin was sitting with his head in his hands. "Everything is going to be okay," he reassured his brother.

Part 2

On Cloud Nine

Anna, the lovely flower plucked much too soon from my garden. Why did she leave me? Can I really make it without her? She gave my life purpose. She calmed my world and handled our home. Kelvin realized that he didn't know how to do a lot of things, but Anna made me feel like he could do anything. Anna has passed away, leaving Kelvin alone to raise their two beautiful children, Dericka, now 11 and Kelvin, Jr, 7. Dericka was a quiet and intuitive little girl, who was so full of confidence and joy until her mother died.

She was beautiful, a perfect mixture of her mother and father, receiving the best features of both parents. Kelvin, Jr, was the spitting image of his mother in male form. Always a ball of activity and full of conversation, Kelvin, Jr was a charismatic young man and adorably

handsome. It has been a couple of weeks since the funeral. Kelvin hadn't been active a couple of weeks since the funeral and Kelvin hadn't left his home; he sat around feeling bad about Anna's death. A couple of his buddies from worked stopped by to pay their respect.

"Hey, Kelvin! Come and take a ride with us!" they yelled at him. "Nah, I don't feel so well," Kelvin yelled back. Dennis said, "Man look here, the reason that you don't feel so well is because you are sitting here feeling sorry for yourself. Look, your wife, Anna would not want you to be lying around here wasting away. You need to get your act together! Your kids are going to need you to get it together. They really need you now." Dennis handed Kelvin a pill. "I used to feel that way when I hurt my back, but I went to this doctor who understood that I needed to keep living. He gave me something that helped me come out of it and I've been back on my feet since. Here, take this. It will make you feel a lot better." Kelvin took the pill and began to watch television. Jimmy said, "Dennis, hey, what did you give him?"

"I just gave him is life back. It is just a pill to make him feel better." Dennis said nonchalantly. Jimmy said, "Man, don't you know that Kelvin is a pastor of a church?!" Dennis grinned and said, "Man, he's going to be okay.

That's all the more reason why he should get himself up and out of this house." Jimmy said, "Look, I'm out of here! I'm not going to hell for letting you give a preacher some drugs." Jimmy pulled off in his car. After thinking about what he had just given Kelvin, Dennis jumped in his car and left right behind him.

Later that evening, Alvin came by to check on Kelvin. Alvin rang the doorbell. Kelvin yelled from the bedroom for him to come in. Kelvin was getting ready to take a shower. "Kelvin, you look like you feel a lot better brother." "Alvin, I feel like I am floating on a cloud".

Alvin said, "Man, you must feel really great!" I told you that all you needed was some good rest." Kelvin began singing as he entered the bathroom to shower. Alvin wondered what was the reason for this all of a sudden change that had come over Kelvin to change his mood so quickly. "Kelvin, if you want, you can ride with me to church."

"Okay," Kelvin replied. "I'll do just that." Kelvin came into the living room showered, shaved and well dressed. Alvin said, "Man, you are sharp!" Alvin asked him. Kelvin wore a navy double breasted suit, soft yellow shirt, diamond cufflinks, a tie with a yellow, blue, and cream paisley design, and camel colored Stacy Adam shoes. "When did you get that tie?" he finished.

"Anna gave it to me for my birthday three months ago". Six feet three inches of a caramel brown complexion, with a square jaw, high cheekbones, and a head full of gray hair, the sixteen years as a foreman in the manufacturing industry had chiseled his body and although he was a little soft around the middle, Kelvin was a handsome and appealing gentleman. He was checking himself out in the mirror and he couldn't stop from admiring what he saw in that mirror. He felt as if he was preparing to go on stage at some R&B music concert as a headliner. For the first time in what felt like too long of a time, he felt alive and tingly all over. The numbness of grief that had been weighing him down like an anchor around his neck had magically disappeared. Alvin looked at him and said, "Ok, snap out of it! We'll be late if you continue this one-man fashion show."

Kelvin seemed to be in another world as he kept staring into the mirror and didn't move. Alvin walked over to him and touched him. It shook him. Kelvin replied, "What do you want?" Alvin asked, "Man, are you alright? Kelvin looked back at him like he could see through him,

"Yeah, I feel great, why?" Alvin's voice lowered, "Kelvin, you were just staring in the mirror for five minutes without blinking an eye, that's why. Maybe you need to stay home tonight and rest." Kelvin said, "What am I supposed to tell my members?"

Alvin cleared his throat, "Call them and tell them you can't make it; tell them you aren't well yet." Kelvin looked down at his clothing, "Well, that would be a lie and I can't do that, Alvin." Upon arriving to church, Alvin took his seat on the deacons' bench. Kelvin went into the pastor's study. As he got ready for tonight's message, he caught himself just standing in a daze again. "What is wrong with me? I am feeling a little funny" he said to no one at all.

In the sanctuary, the choir began to sing the praise and worship *"Send Down The Latter Rain."* Located in the middle of the city, on one of the oldest streets in town, the church stood as an architectural monument. Three stories high with stained glass windows flown in specifically from France and columns imported from Italy at the entrance of the arched walkways that led to the oak double doors with unique, handmade carvings of well-known Bible figures. The church was a regular meeting place for local leaders during the Civil Rights Era. Inside, folks stood up and sang along with the choir. The Holy Spirit was moving all over the church. Sister Drake got up and started doing her Holy Spirit dance. Once Sister Tamla saw Sister Drake dancing, she began her holy dance too. The spirit was high in the church and just about all of the members were experiencing the move of the Spirit.

The deacon stood to begin the consecration and responsive reading signaling to the congregation that it was time for the sermon to be delivered. Kelvin entered the sanctuary from the study and went up to the pulpit. The congregation started clapping and praising the Lord even more. Kelvin grabbed the microphone and started preaching. He was moving all over the place as if he couldn't be still. He mumbled his words and behaved very strangely. He ultimately started laughing uncontrollably; causing Alvin and several other deacons to run up to him to help him out of the pulpit and back to the pastor's study. A doctor was called and after he examined Kelvin he concluded that all Kelvin needed was some rest. He shook his head as Kelvin appeared to be showing all the symptoms of having symptoms of post-traumatic stress syndrome or under some sort of reaction to medication. He deduced it was probably due to the death of his wife and brother occurring so close to each other.

"Is he going to be alright, doctor?" Alvin asked Dr. Sessan. "Alvin, what did Kelvin take?" Doctor Sessan responded. Alvin was confused. "What are you saying, Dr. Sessan?" he asked. "By the look of his eyes, he has been taking some kind of drugs."

"Doctor, you are wrong, my brother would never take any drugs. Don't be telling anyone else that either. You know my brother is a pastor of this church and four others." Alvin firmly stated to Dr. Sessan.

Dr. Sessan, an elderly veteran doctor, rubbed his balding gray head and said, "Son it's my job to let you know what's going on with your brother so I told you. Now whether you believe me or not, that's the truth". Dr. Sessan grabbed his things. "I have more things to do, so I have to go." Alvin composed himself, apologized for his outburst and asked the doctor to please use empathize with his brother's situation. He then escorted Dr. Sessan to his car and watched him drive off.

Alvin was embarrassed and furious with his brother. He returned to check on Kelvin and found him lying on the sofa in the pastor's study. "Kelvin, are you okay," he asked him. Kelvin looked up puzzled and replied, "What are you talking about, Alvin?"

"So you don't remember what happened in church today?" Alvin detailed to Kelvin how he had been acting during service. "Brother, I have been on the street for many years. I know what people act like when they are on drugs and that's exactly what you were acting like today."

Kelvin put his head in his hands trying to remember what could have gone wrong. Then like a rocket, it came back to him. "Well…earlier today Dennis came by to check on me. I explained how I was feeling and he told me he was like that before and he gave me a pill. He told me it would help me relax and feel a lot better. I took it and just like he said, it made me feel a lot better. It took a lot of things off my mind."

Alvin could not believe what he was hearing. His tea tootling brother had taken a drug without question from Dennis of all people. Everyone knew that Dennis was a walking prescription drug cabinet. "In the future, Kelvin, please don't take just anything someone gives you." In Dennis's defense, Kelvin stated, "But he is one of my buddies from work, he didn't mean any harm." Alvin loved that his brother refused to see the worse in anyone. "Like I said, don't accept pills from anyone, even good ol' boy Dennis, okay?" Alvin stated firmly.

As he stood to leave, Alvin added, "Let's get you home, Kelvin." Kelvin felt that Alvin was overreacting and shrugged off his warning. As he prepared for bed after he got home, Kelvin continued to think about how good the pill Dennis gave him made him feel. He knew that he definitely wanted some more of that good feeling.

Kelvin began hanging out with his work buddies and was having fun, getting high and forgetting that he was a father and a pastor of a church. Kelvin would hang out all late with the guys after work and had a babysitter watching his children. Over eight months had passed and Kelvin still hadn't gotten himself together. Church members begin to question Alvin about Kelvin's whereabouts. There were reports from members saying they had seen the pastor late nights partying in the night clubs and the congregation wanted to know what was really going on with Kelvin.

"We cannot just hold his pastor position forever while he is absent because he is out gallivanting," touted Head Deacon Tann. We may need to have to vote and get ourselves another pastor. We have given him plenty of time to get his act together. You know the main thing is the rumors and allegation we are hearing."

Alvin said, "Have you all called him, Deacon Tann?" Deacon Tann, lowered his voice, "Look, Alvin, I have called Pastor Kelvin numerous times but he doesn't ever pick up the phone! I will try to call him again because tonight we will have the hearing about whether he stays or goes."

Kelvin was voted out as pastor during the church meeting. Alvin went home and told his wife Gail that Kelvin was not the pastor anymore and had been voted out. "Alvin, how did you vote?" she asked him. "I voted for what was best for the church," he replied.

"I know it was a hard decision, but you had a commitment to fulfill, you are on the deacon board," she reasoned. "How about we ride down to Kelvin's house and check up on the kids?" When they made it there, Kelvin's car was there, and as they walked up to the door, it was open so they walked in. There were dirty dishes in the sink and filthy clothes were thrown all over the house.

They went in the back bedroom and found the kids lying in filth, burning up with fever. Gail watched the children as Alvin went through the house looking for Kelvin, but he could not find him. Alvin and Gail took Dericka and Kelvin Jr. to the emergency room. During the emergency room visit, the children were given some medicine and discharged them. Gail said, "What are we going to do with these kids?" We will keep them until Kelvin gets back home".

When Kelvin came home later on that night, he found a letter Alvin left for him. Angry and high, Kelvin called Alvin. "Why did you take my kids?! Oh…now you want my kids, too! After you all holier than thou voted me out of the church, now you are all in my house taking my kids? Is that it?" Kelvin screamed into his side of the phone. "Alvin, I knew it all these years that you hated being in my shadow. I know you couldn't wait to see me crumble and fall." Alvin was horrified, "That's not right, Kelvin. I have always loved you even when I was strung out on drugs and alcohol just like you are now. You need to go and get some professional help. Look I know exactly what is happening with you. Don't wait until it is too late!"

Kelvin said, "What? Are the professionals going to help me bring back my mother, my wife, and my brother?" Alvin said, "No man, but they can help you get yourself back on track again." Kelvin said, "I'll pass. You know, I don't feel no pain when I am getting high. Alvin, I feel good when I am high."

"Okay, Kelvin, but what about when the high is gone? You are back to your old self," Alvin asked. "You need to worry about bringing my kids back to my house and that's it!" Kelvin hung up the phone. Alvin said, "Gail, let's get these kids back to his house." Kelvin was standing at the door when Alvin and Gail pulled up with the children. Alvin walked them to the door.

Kelvin said, "Thank you, but if you want to do me a favor, please mind your own business okay?" The kids ran up to Kelvin and gave him a hug and kiss. Dericka waved at Alvin as he left. Alvin sadly waved back. Gail said, "I hope that you are not going to stop checking on your nephew and niece just because of this." "Gail, you know me better than that, I'll check on them every day." Alvin said. Dericka saw her Uncle Alvin as a super hero.

She had been so worried about her brother. She had been feeling bad since they had eaten the food that had been left in the refrigerator. She didn't know how old it was, but their little stomachs had been aching so bad from hunger that she thought it couldn't make them feel worse than they already did. She was wrong. How should she warm the food for them? Or care for them? Dericka had so many questions and no one was there to answer them for her. Just when she learned how to pop popcorn, the microwave had quit working. This happened as they tried to warm up something that was wrapped in aluminum foil 3weeks ago. Their dad had not even noticed that it was no longer working. After about an hour or so after eating, Kelvin Jr had been vomiting and sweating as if he had been swimming or standing in the shower. She saw his eyes roll in the back of his head two or three times before Uncle Alvin had showed up, but she was too weak and sick to get up to check on him. The last thing she remembered before drifting off to sleep was talking to her mother, praying that she would ask God to send them an angel to save them.

When she woke up, her Aunt Gail and Uncle Alvin were there. She silently thanked her mom and thanked God for listening to her. Where was their Daddy? Why did he keep leaving them? Why didn't he love them anymore? What had they done to their Dad that he didn't want to be them? Or care for them? Dericka had so many questions she wished someone would answer for her, but she was too scared to ask anyone because they just might have the answers that would separate her from her little brother.

Months went by and Kelvin got worse. Some nights he wouldn't even come home. Alvin was busy and tired from working two jobs and he didn't check up on the kids a routinely as he did at first. Little Kelvin would be at home crying because there was no food in the house.

One day Dericka had enough and wanted to do something to help her little brother get food. She told Kelvin Jr, "Stay here at the house, I am going to the store to get us something to eat and drink." She walked to the grocery store and stole some hotdogs, candy bars, and soda. She was so scared and thought that she'd be struck dead by a lightning bolt before she made it home. She was angry with her father for making her have to steal so that she and her brother could eat. She prayed and asked God to forgive her. She told her Mama that she was sorry. She will never forget the look on her brother's face when she walked in with the food from the grocery store. He looked so happy. She had not seen him smile like that in a while. His temporary joy made her crime worth whatever she may have to face because of it. They laughed together as they found something to watch on TV.

Dericka and Kelvin Jr. ate very well that night, until their bellies were full and then went to sleep. This was the first time in weeks that they were able to sleep without their stomachs growling from hunger. Dericka felt like she had done a great job taking care of her brother today. She knew that she would have to continue being a good big sister by doing whatever she had to do so that her brother had what he needed. She prayed over the food and even though she knew she was wrong for stealing, she felt like she did not have any other options. Her Daddy continued to leave her and her brother home alone. It's like they did not exist to him anymore. They had died to him just like their Mama did.

Oh, how Dericka missed her Mama. She felt the pain of her Mama's absence every day. She could not understand what she or her brother could have ever done so wrong to end up in a predicament like this. A dead mother and a drug addict for a father who didn't care if they live or died. Dericka looked at her little brother and decided she would be strong for him. She assured Kelvin Jr., "Little brother, don't worry, I'll take care of you. You won't be hungry anymore, you just watch and see."

On the nights when Dericka couldn't steal any food, she would go out at late hours after the restaurants closed and get food that had been thrown away into the big dumpsters behind the restaurants and bring it home to eat. She began to regularly go to the dumpster of a local pizza place. She and Kelvin Jr. would eat thrown away pizza and bread sticks. One day, as the manager reviewed the restaurant's video surveillance for the month, he saw a little girl go over into the dumpster and come back out with food. He saw her put it into a back sack and take off running down the road. As he continued reviewing the footage, the manager witnessed that every night she went into the dumpster to get food. The manager began to cry; this little girl couldn't have been any more than ten or eleven years of age. He called one of his cooks to come and look at the video and told him to sit the food they threw away by the back door from now on rather than throw it in the dumpster. The same evening that the manager was viewing the tape of the little girl taking food out of the dumpster, Dericka was on a mission to feed herself and her brother. Dericka went back to the grocery store, this time she hid two sodas under her t- shirt. When she got to the door, both sodas fell from under her clothes. She took off running, but the security guard grabbed her before she could get out of the door. She was taken to the back office.

"What's your name, little girl? Why did you try to steal those drinks?" She was scared to death. "I am thirsty and my brother is at home alone and he is thirsty too. I must get back home to my little brother before he wakes up and sees that I am gone," she said sheepishly. The security guard said, "The police are on their way to get you and carry you home." The police arrived and took Dericka home.

When they knocked on the door, Dericka said, "No one is home except my little brother and me." Officer Tim Reid asked, "Where are your parents, young lady?" Dericka replied, "My daddy is at work and my mother is dead." The officer asked her, "Don't you have a sitter, little girl?" Dericka didn't answer; she just shook her head to say, "No."

The officer left a telephone number on a card that he stuck in the door that stated Social Services had taken custody of the children. When Kelvin made it home later that day, he was high. When he walked up to the door and saw the note from the officer, he began to cry because he knew deep in his heart that he had lost his kids. Social Services called him every day and left messages, but Kelvin refused to call them back. Kelvin's drug and alcohol addiction started affecting his job, as he would miss days from work without any valid excuses.

Saved By Cancer

A few days ago, Kelvin's boss came up to him and informed him how his performance had been very slack the past year. He had worked there for so long his boss had covered for him as much as he could, but now it was affecting the morale of the entire department. Kelvin had spiraled to a bad place and no one could reach him to bring him out of it. His boss explained that the word came from the corporate office, he must let him go. The boss told Kelvin that although he was being terminated, he could still receive his health benefits and 401K.

As the weeks went by, from time to time Kelvin would come out of stupor long enough to give a few moments of thought about his kids. He sincerely wondered how they were doing and where they were living. Kelvin was doing really bad; he wasn't taking showers or washing his clothes. His family wouldn't come around him anymore because when they did, Kelvin would beg them for money. Kelvin checked his mailbox one day and read a notice that he had five days left to vacate his home. He stopped paying bills months ago.

Meanwhile, Dericka, and Kelvin Jr. were staying at a foster home outside of town. Dericka would fight every day to protect her little brother from being picked on. Kelvin Jr. would cry and scream that he wanted his daddy. He was placed in isolation by himself until he would stop crying. Four years had passed, Dericka was going on fifteen years old and Kelvin Jr. was eleven. The kids decided that they had to depend on themselves and realized that they may never see their father again. Their teachers loved them because they were very well mannered and smart. Uncle Alvin would come and visit them almost every other day.

During one of his visits Dericka asked, "Why haven't you ever come for us and taken us to stay with you Uncle?" Alvin said, "Your daddy told me not to get you. He even wrote a letter to Social Services saying that he didn't want me to raise ya'll. I know it wasn't him talking. It was the drugs and alcohol making him behave that way, but it was his wishes."

Kelvin Jr. said, "Uncle Alvin, I know that you love us and I know that our daddy does too. We love you Uncle Alvin and I pray for you and my daddy every night. You are a great uncle." Alvin grabbed both of them, hugged them, and said, "I love you too." He cried and prayed the entire trip home. He was so torn about what had happened to Kelvin and his family.

Kelvin, having lost his children, lost his home, and lost his job, begin staying in bars until they closed and then wander the streets, looking for places where he could get high. He made a home from one place to the next, rarely even remembering how he got wherever he ended up. Kelvin left town, drifting further and further south and his path led him to Atlanta. He was content to live there on the streets. So long as Kelvin could get high, he could handle his circumstances no matter how grim. Kelvin was sleeping just about anywhere he could lay his head, mostly in abandoned houses that had been boarded up by the city. He would eat at the mission or go behind restaurants and get food out of the dumpster after closing hours.

While on the streets, Kelvin had witnessed some strange things and met some decent people. The street people for the most part, looked out for one another and shared what they had when they had it to share. Kelvin was sometimes amazed, as he would think back on his pastoring days; there were times when he couldn't get Christians in the church to speak to or sit by one another, let alone share what they had with one another.

Dwight was a person that he had met on the streets. Kelvin felt that Dwight was better than some of the church folk that Kelvin had known for years. Dwight was grateful and appreciative; he was humble and always had a good attitude. Whenever there was a dispute and Dwight was around, he would always be the peacemaker, even when the incident did not concern him. He had a way of bringing people together.

One Tuesday night, Kelvin was lying down asleep in an old abandoned house. A man came walking through the house looking in and checking every room but some kind of way he didn't see Kelvin. The man went back outside and he returned with a roll of carpet. The man set the roll of carpet in the back room and as he was leaving, Kelvin turned over a lamp. The man stopped and ran to the room where he heard the noise with a gun in his hand. When he got to the room, Kelvin was gone. The man looked around the room again and then he left. As soon as Kelvin heard the man's pickup truck pull off, he climbed down from the ceiling.

Kelvin walked through the house from room to room until he saw the roll of carpet. Kelvin begin to roll out the carpet to see what was in it. As the carpet unrolled, he saw that a dead body was in it. Kelvin jumped back and as he looked at the body, he noticed that the dead man lying in the carpet was his best friend Dwight. Dwight had been beaten in his head and all over his body really bad. As Kelvin looked closer, he saw where Dwight's eye socket had been beaten out. Kelvin was upset and afraid; he did not know what to do, so he grabbed his clothes and went to stay somewhere else. As he was headed out the door, Kelvin spotted a black pickup truck sitting just outside the house. Kelvin took off running and the man in the black pickup saw him and started to follow him in the truck. Kelvin ran for his life. He went down a dark alley and hid behind a trashcan. The man in the pickup slowed down and got out of his truck and began walking down the alley. Kelvin saw the man coming toward him. As Kelvin was lying there he started praying to God. All of a sudden, a police car stopped by the alley and the officer shined his light on the man's vehicle. The man turned and began to walk back toward his vehicle. The police asked, "Is everything okay?"

The big tall dark man, who had just minutes before dumped a dead body in an abandoned house replied, "Yes, officer. Everything is just fine." "You can't block this alley so I am going to need you to move your vehicle." The man got into his truck and pulled off as the officer shined his flashlight back down the alley once more towards the direction Kelvin was hiding. Later that night, Kelvin left that area to lay under the bridge where most of his friends slept. Kelvin lived under the bridge for a couple of years.

Kelvin begin to notice some things about himself. He was getting a lot older. He also noticed that his steps were getting slower and his wind was getting shorter. Kelvin decided to go down to the free health clinic and he was able to get in for a checkup. The doctor, who was obviously disgusted by Kelvin's appearance when he entered the examination room, ordered the nurse to help Kelvin go and clean himself in the restroom.

"I am not going to touch this man nor am I going to sit here and make myself nauseous smelling his filth. Help him to go clean up to improve his personal hygiene as best he can…please!" The doctor hurriedly left the room leaving the nurse and Kelvin alone. Kelvin was mortified. For the first time it really hit him how low he had allowed himself to sink into his despondence. He likened himself to the Prodigal Son that he had preached about so fervently from Gospel of Luke (Luke 15:11-32). Just like that wayward son, Kelvin came to himself in the pig sty of living life in the underworld.

The nurse showed Kelvin where the men's restrooms was and let him get cleaned up. When he returned to the examination room, he was seen by the doctor. They took x-rays of Kelvin's chest and did a complete blood workup. As the doctor looked the test results over, he said, "Kelvin, it is a good thing that came in when you did. There is a spot on your lungs. It doesn't look good. I will send these charts and result off to the lab so that the specialists can take a closer look. I should get them back from the lab in about a week. I will be getting in touch with you in eight days. In the meantime, take these medicine samples, they may help you."

Kelvin took the samples and left the clinic. He began to worry about what the doctor said about the spot on his lung. Kelvin knew that he didn't have any one to turn to if he got sick. He thought about his family and realized that he hadn't talked to any of them family in so many years.

Meanwhile, four more years had passed. Dericka and Kelvin Jr. had matured so fast. In fact, Dericka had grown up, graduated from high school, and she gotten a job right after graduation. She worked and saved her money for an apartment. The first thing she had to do once she secured a job and apartment was to go back to social services for Kelvin Jr. She had to get him out of the foster care system. He was now fifteen.

Dericka worked hard every day to keep a roof over their heads and food on their table. Kelvin Jr. went to school and studied hard, and received excellent grades. A couple of years later, Kelvin Jr. graduates high school and he plans to go away to college.

Once he was in college, Kelvin Jr. found a part time job at a hospital working in the computer lab. Dericka called every day to check on her little brother and see how he was doing with his classes. Kelvin said, "Dericka, college is a lot different from high school." Dericka encouraged Kelvin Jr. "Lil' brother, you can handle it, you are the brains in this family." Kelvin said, "Sis, I don't know, this work is pretty hard." Dericka said, "What is it?

Is anyone up there messing with you? If they are let me know. I will come up there and bust them up." Kelvin Jr. laughed and said, "Look sis, you cannot be beating up everyone for me, by the way it is not anyone messing with me like that. I am sort of in love with this girl that is in my class."

Dericka said, "Oh, my little brother is in love!" Kelvin said, "Be quiet sister don't tell anyone." Dericka said, "Does she know you are still a virgin?" Kelvin Jr. said, "No, and don't tell the whole world okay?!" Dericka started to laugh. Kelvin, Jr. said, "You got your laugh for today but I have to go and study now. I will talk to you later monkey mouth and don't tell anyone about what I told you, please."

During this time, their father was still on the streets hanging with his friends, stripping abandoned houses for copper, brass, and aluminum. Taking it to the junk yards for cash. Kelvin's health had really gotten bad. He looked at himself in the mirror one day and he began to shed tears. His hair was getting long and gray, and his jaws were sinking in from all the teeth that had fallen out due to his drug use. His back and shoulders had begun to slump. Kelvin had been in the streets for more years than he could remember.

The streets had taken from what it was owed. It had taken its toll on Kelvin and had really gotten the best of him. Kelvin tried to go to rehab but he always seems to end back out in the streets. While sitting down talking to one of his friends one day, a man walked over to them and started handing out Bibles.

The man asked Kelvin and his friends, "Do you know Jesus?" Kelvin's friends said, "Yeah, we know Him and I am sitting here enjoying Him right now with this bottle of E&J brandy." They howled with laughter. "Hey, that is not nice to say," Kelvin told his friends. Woodrow said, "Oh, I guess now you're saved all of a sudden because the preacher man done come by."

Kelvin said, "It's not that, it is called having respect for God's people." The preacher man said, "Hey, you can't be who I think you are?! Oh my Lord, it is you!" Woodrow said, "This preacher man is crazy, he thinks you are Jesus!" The preacher said, "No, I am not crazy and I don't have him mistaken for Jesus." The preacher continued. "I know who you are and maybe it is a reason you are here. I am not the one to judge you, take my number Kelvin, and if there is anything you need just call me anytime." He handed his card to Kelvin. Kelvin put it in his shirt pocket.

Woodrow said, "Man, I am standing here too! Oh, you don't see me, huh? I bet you if I robbed you, you'd recognize me." The preacher acted as if he didn't even hear Woodrow and kept talking to Kelvin. "My name is Bishop Shepherd and I am the pastor of Jerusalem Baptist Church. Kelvin, if you wouldn't mind, I would love for you to come and worship with us some time. You can be my special guest."

Kelvin said, "Bishop, in my heart, I would love to visit, but look at me! I am a crack head junkie and an alcoholic. I can't go into God's house like this." The Bishop said, "Kelvin, I once heard you preach a sermon called, "You are never too far to come back home." You know, that sermon was on fire! You need to check yourself, because even though you preached that sermon years ago you were talking about yourself. You were right too, Kelvin, you are never too far to come back home. Please try to make it to church Sunday if you can and bring your friend, Woodrow." "Preacher man, he don't have to bring me, humph! I have legs and I can use them too. Watch me use them to go across the street to the liquor store." Woodrow said as he left. "Like I said Kelvin or Pastor Kelvin, please come and join us this Sunday if you can, okay?" Later on that night, as Kelvin was lying down, his body was telling him to go and get something to make him feel good.

Kelvin was trying to fight it, but the urge and temptation was too hard for him. Kelvin started to get up and then he thought about what the Bishop had said earlier. Kelvin fell down to his knees and started praying. He began to have a talk with Jesus and he began to pour his heart out to Him. Kelvin's words were, "Father, I know I have failed you over and over again all these long years. And Father, I have taken this heavy load upon myself for so many years. And Father, I know for a fact that when I was in trouble and I was too stubborn to call upon Your Name, You still pulled me through and kept me out of harm's way. So Father, help me to get back on my feet again, Dear Father. And, I shall serve You and only You Father. Father, I know when my mom died while I was a young age, I felt weak and then my brother, whom I truly loved died." Sobbing, Kelvin continued. "And then, Lord, when You took my darling wife, Anna, away, I really fell by the wayside. Father, You know that I am sick and that I can't get well. And, all I want Father, is to be Your humble servant just one more time. Father I have two wonderful kids somewhere out there and I know they are grown and probably have families of their own by now, but Father, I would just love to see them again. I hope they would love to see me, too. So Heavenly Father, please just let me see my babies, Lord, just one more time." Then Kelvin remembered this song he would always sing when he was feeling down and all alone.

He started singing this song called *"Yes, Jesus Loves Me."* Kelvin's eyes had filled up with water and he just couldn't hold back his tears so he was crying while he sung. Kelvin held up his hands to God and fell back on his knees. He asked God for forgiveness and strength to make it through. As Kelvin remained on his knees, Woodrow looked over, and saw him praying and crying. Woodrow threw away his E&J bottle, fell down on his knees and began to pray, as well.

Woodrow asked God for forgiveness of his sins and told God that he was a sinner. He stated he needed God to touch him and heal him as well. Woodrow was telling God how he was a walking dead man. He told God that he wasn't ready to die yet. He told God that he wanted to be saved and he was tired of living out on the streets like an animal. He told God how cold it gets in the winter and how hot it gets in the summer staying in an abandoned house. He cried out, "Lord, Lord I am tired. Cancer is all over my body and I ache every day and I can't afford no treatment. Lord, I don't have the right kind of insurance so the doctors send me back on the streets to die! Lord, it makes me so bitter with people today; mankind has turned their backs on me." Kelvin had overheard Woodrow's prayer. After Woodrow finished Kelvin walked over and gave Woodrow a hug. "What was that hug for, Kelvin?" Woodrow asked. Kelvin said, "I overheard your prayer to God and everyone didn't turn their backs on you. I am still here. "Father, I am asking that You heal him as well." Woodrow, I was telling God how He has been your Friend and always will be." Woodrow smiled and said, "Kelvin let's help each other out and get clean."

He added, "Listen here, Woodrow, this voyage isn't going to be a walk in the park, it is going to be all kind of temptation ahead of us with these drugs and alcohol".

Woodrow said, "I know it is going to be hard, but I at least want to try." Kelvin said, "Good, that is all a man can do is try. If God see we are trying, he will do the rest." The next day, Kelvin and Woodrow went and admitted themselves into a rehab. They talked and was filling out paperwork and the lady at the desk said, "Kelvin Johnson you back again?!"

Kelvin proudly said, "Yes, I am and I brought a friend. His name is Woodrow." The lady replied, "Kelvin, I hope you are not just coming here for a warm bed and food again." Kelvin said, "No, I am not. I want to be free of what has taken a hold on me all these years." Mrs. Joyce said, "I have heard that so many times before. All of you just come in here and take what the system gives you for free and then you all are gone. I hope this time you are for real because I am so tired of seeing you milk the system".

Kelvin said, "This time I am here to stay. I am not quitting this time!" Joyce looked at Woodrow and said, "What you standing there looking all crazy for. What about you? Are you here to play games or are you here for real?" Woodrow said, "Like Kelvin said, we are here to take this rehab class and get on with our lives, we are tired of you all looking down on us and treating us like we are animals when we are not." Woodrow and Kelvin finished the filling out the papers they got from Mrs. Joyce and she showed Kelvin and Woodrow to their rooms.

Kelvin told Woodrow, "Well, we must be going to different rehabs because they got me here and they have you about ten miles down the road." Woodrow said, "I don't care, just as long as I have me a nice warm bed and a hot meal every day." Kelvin said, "Man, see, that's what Joyce was talking about. She said that the only reason we were here was to get a place to stay and have a hot meal". They both laughed. Woodrow walked with Kelvin to his rehab center and Kelvin waved good bye.

The Battle For Restoration

As the day passed, Kelvin's demons tried to take control of him. Kelvin was trying to get rid of it, but his demon just would not go away. Kelvin would be balled up in a corner in his bed and Joyce would come by and check on him and bring him his food and drink. Joyce asked Kelvin did he want her to give him some medicine to help him heal and Kelvin replied, "No, I can fight it, I have to fight! I cannot let Satan win the victory over my body anymore. Satan, I rebuke you in the name of Jesus!"

Joyce saw that Kelvin did not want his medicine so she took it away. Weeks went by and Kelvin was still suffering from withdrawal and his demons were still bothering him, but Kelvin continued to fight it. Kelvin's body was so weak from not eating. He was vomiting and not putting food back in his body. Kelvin had lost an enormous amount of weight but he still kept on fighting. One night, Kelvin seen this man in his room he was so weak and could hardly see him, but Kelvin heard the man's voice. Kelvin said, "Who are you and what are you doing in my room?" The voice told Kelvin, "I am your friend and I go by many names." Kelvin said, "State what you want and leave me alone." The man said, "I come here today to help you get well." Kelvin said, "How can you help me?"

The strange man opened his hand and he had some drugs in it and he opened his jacket and he had needles and all sorts of things. Kelvin's eyes got big. The man said, "Come over to me and get whatever you desire." Kelvin was walking over towards the man and just as Kelvin was getting ready to take the items, Joyce knocked on his door. "Kelvin Johnson, are you okay in there?"

Kelvin snapped out of it and yelled, "Yes, I am okay now!"

Joyce left and the man said, "Look, you better come over here and get what you need, this is your last chance." Kelvin said, "I know who you are now. You can't fool me; you come around to feed off of my weakness, but today is not going to be your day because Satan I rebuke you in the name of Jesus! Satan, get behind me in the name of Jesus!"

Satan's image vanished from Kelvin's room. Four months passed and Kelvin was doing much better, the worst was behind him. Kelvin was going to class every day. Joyce came to him and said, "Kelvin, I am so proud of you, you really fooled me this time. I thought you were going to do like you had always done before but who am I to judge?" Joyce said, "You are doing so well, I'd like to let you know about a dentist down the street who does dental work on rehab patients for free. Go and see him tomorrow, he will be coming here to the center." Kelvin was very happy to hear he could get his teeth repaired. He said, "I sure will, I need my mouth fixed."

Joyce said, "Cool, just don't smile until you get them fixed okay? Two more months went by and it was time for Kelvin to graduate from rehab. Kelvin had been so busy trying to do the right things that he remembered how much he had forgotten all about his friend, Woodrow. Kelvin smiled to himself and thought, I just hope Woodrow has done just as well. Kelvin walked up to the front desk and asked Joyce how his friend Woodrow was doing.

Joyce tried not to look sad, but she said, "Woodrow did not make it Kelvin. Kelvin was shocked! "Well why? Did he drop out? What happened?" Joyce said, "He did not drop out Kelvin. Woodrow was having real bad withdrawals; he wouldn't let us give him any medicine just like you had done. We honored that for two weeks and he just wasn't getting any better, so we tried to get him to take some medication but Woodrow said he wanted to get clean drug free. The nurse went by the next morning to see how Woodrow was doing. She called for him but he did not answer. When she went in to check on him, he was dead." Kelvin fell to his knees and started to cry. Joyce rose to her feet to comfort him. She whispered, "Woodrow died exactly like he wanted to, he was drug free. He just refused to take his medicine." Joyce asked Kelvin, "Did you know that Woodrow had cancer?" Kelvin said, "I overheard him praying to God about it one day and that's how I found out." "Yes, he had cancer all over his body and he should not have tried to go cold turkey in the condition he was in. It was too much for his body to take at once." Kelvin said, "Every man has a reason for what they do." Joyce said, "I reckon you are right. Kelvin, what are you going to do when you leave rehab?" "I am going to find me some work," he replied. Joyce told Kelvin that she had a number he could call to help him find some work. The day came for Kelvin to graduate from the program. He left the rehab and got a job working for a construction company. Kelvin rented a room at a hotel located in downtown Atlanta which made it convenient for Kelvin to get back and forth to work on the bus line. Kelvin was on his job for a couple of weeks when he received his first paycheck. Kelvin would pay his room up for a whole month and whatever he had left he would save. Every night as Kelvin would go to sleep he would hear his neighbors partying next door, to the point that he was not able to sleep. One night, someone knocked on his door and Kelvin got up and answered the door. He opened the door and there was a lady standing there with sleazy night wear on. "You got a light?" she asked. Kelvin said, "I do not smoke anymore and just got out of rehab not too long ago." "My name is Carla and I am just looking to have some fun for tonight. You think you can come out and play?" "I am not looking for any kind of fun, Miss Lady. But maybe you can try next door. If you don't mind, Miss I would like to get some sleep please." Carla said, "I will leave you alone if you will just give me some sex." "Miss, could you please go and bother someone else, I am not interested." She pulled out a crack pipe and Kelvin's eyes lit up. "I know you want a hit, just give me a light. I will let you hit it and I will let you hit something else, too."

Kelvin remembered how Satan tried to attack him while he was weak in rehab. Kelvin looked at the woman Kelvin said, "I do not smoke anymore. I just got out of rehab. He actually thought he saw the devil all in her eyes. Kelvin said, "Satan, I rebuke you in the name of Jesus!" She left and Kelvin shut his door. He laid back down and got his rest.

Eventually, Kelvin met Casandra, a lady who lived at the same hotel. Kelvin and Casandra became really close friends. One Sunday, while at breakfast, Casandra asked Kelvin, "Look Kelvin, you seem like you are a very good man, why don't you go to church?" "I have been thinking about going but I just don't know how. I'll have you know, it has been over twenty years since I have stepped into a church house," he replied.

"Well, I attend a pretty decent church and they treat me okay. Why don't you come and go with me today as my guest, please?" she asked. "Sure," Kelvin relented. He had been out of God's House long enough. It was time to go back. They rode the bus to church together. When they got off the bus, Kelvin looked around and said, "This is the church you go to?"

"Yes," she replied. They walked up the steps and went inside the door where the members greeted them. One of the deacons asked Casandra, "Who is this, your friend?" Kelvin spoke up and said, "My name is Kelvin Johnson." The gentleman with the deep voice replied, "Well, now.

Welcome to Jerusalem Baptist Church of Atlanta, GA, Mr. Kelvin Johnson. I am Deacon John." He shook Kelvin's hand. The preacher stood up and said, "The sermon for today is "I've Been In The Storm Too Long." Kelvin squinted his eyes and looked at the preacher. He thought to himself, I know that preacher. Kelvin asked Casandra, "Is his name Bishop Shepherd?" "Yes. How do you know my Bishop?" she asked. Kelvin smiled and said, "It is a long story." The Bishop preached the sermon. The choir sang hymns that pierced the souls of the saints. The church was lit up praising God, literally, over half of the church was actively praising God.

Kelvin was so amazed at the Bishop because that was the sermon that he made up and preached on over twenty years ago, Kelvin was so happy to know that the message he preached over twenty years ago still had that effect on people. So the Bishop finished preaching and he asked if anyone want to be saved or want God to heal them of what man say is impossible. Casandra grabbed Kelvin's hand and pulled him up and they walked up for prayer.

Bishop put his hand on Kelvin and said, "My brother, what is it that you want God to do in your life? Then he looked at Kelvin in his face and said, "Oh my Lord! It is you, Kelvin Johnson, God's Servant has come back home! You almost look like your old self!"

Kelvin laughingly said, "It has been over twenty something years."
Bishop announced, "Church, this is Kelvin Johnson and the sermon I preached today I heard him preach it over twenty years ago. The credit is all his. Kelvin said, "No, it is not, the credit goes to God."
Bishop said, "Hallelujah, Hallelujah…praise God from Whom all blessing flow." Then the Bishop started to dance like David. The drum, piano, guitar they all were playing a victory song the Bishop was dancing all over the pulpit. Then Kelvin felt the Holy Spirit came upon him and he began to also praise God like David.

They danced and shouted all over the pulpit and danced and the church was full and they were all on their feet shouting and dancing even Deacon John started shouting. Deacon Larry said, "Out of all my years, I have never seen this church praise God as they are doing today. This man must be a true man of God! Where is he from?" After church turned out, Bishop asked

Kelvin to have dinner with him and his family today. Kelvin said, "I would love to Bishop but I came here on the bus with Casandra." "Well bring her, we have plenty of food for her too, she is welcomed to share dinner with us!"

"Okay, let me go ask her if she'd like to go". Casandra let Kelvin know that she would love to go and have dinner with them. They went to Red Lobster. Everyone ordered and Kelvin pulled Bishop to the side and told him that he did not know they were going to Red Lobster's to eat and that he could not afford to pay their tab. The Bishop laughed and explained that if he invited him to eat, it was customary that the person who issued the invitation paid the tab. With that being said he said to Kelvin, "Don't worry, I got everyone's tab." Kelvin thanked him for that. Get used to it Pastor Kelvin. When you maintain the right relationship with your Heavenly Father, blessing will chase you."

After everyone ate, Deacon John asked Bishop, "Who are our guests, really?" He was not about to allow his unanswered question remain unanswered. Kelvin looked at Deacon John and the Bishop stood up and said, "This man is a true man of God that has been through a storm and he just finally found his way out. I would love for Kelvin to join our church. You know if it had not been for the sermon I heard him preach years ago, I probably would not have been where I am today. I know what it feels like going through something too because I have not always been saved. You know life has challenges and life has its ups and downs and we really don't know what a storm really is until we have been through one and this man Kelvin Johnson he has been there so judge not unless we want to be judged." In front of everyone the Bishop asked Kelvin, "Do you want to become my assistant pastor at this church?" He saw that Kelvin did not know what to say. "Go home and think it over and get back with me."

As Kelvin and Casandra rode the bus back to the hotel, Casandra asked Kelvin, "Who are you, seriously?" Casandra asked. "I am just a man." He answered. "Are you a preacher?" she asked. "Once upon a time, I was," he replied. "You must have been a powerful preacher the way the Bishop talks about you." She said, smiling.

Kelvin's face turned dark, ask he spoke…"I only did my job, saying what God put into my mouth to speak. But one day I fell weak. I took my eyes off of God and I fell to the wayside. Then my life did a 360° turn around and I lost everything I had. If I had only practiced what I was preaching to the saints. Yes, I lost my dad, my mom, my brother Andrew, and my wife Anna. I lost my pastoral leadership, my job, and both of my little babies." Casandra was surprised, "You have kids?"

"Yes, I do, but I have not heard from them in over twenty years," He answered. "Why, Kelvin? Why so long?" Casandra asked. "Because I have been in the streets so long that I lost contact with them, and my brother and all of my sisters," was his answer. Casandra said, "You almost sound like Job from the Bible." For the first time, Kelvin thought about his situation. "You just do not know how it hurts inside knowing that you do not have anyone to love," he said in retrospect. "Kelvin, you have me. I will always be your friend and you have Jesus. He will never leave you nor forsake you," Casandra reminded him. That made Kelvin smiled. "You know what? You are right," he said.

Ladies and Gentlemen, Pastor Kevin

When they made it back to the hotel, the Bishop called Kelvin. Bishop Shepherd told him that he needed to go out of town tomorrow due to an unforeseen emergency. He would appreciate it if while he was away if Kelvin will fill in as his speaker.

Kelvin said, "Bishop, I do not know what time I am going to get off of work tomorrow." "Pastor Kelvin, if you want a job working in the church, go to work tomorrow and give your boss a notice and I will pay your salary every week. I also have a nice three-bedroom house for you that comes with the position, if you decide it is the position for you. You can move in right away if you accept the job," Bishop Shepherd told him.

Kelvin could not believe the blessing he was given. "Sir, I never liked doing construction work anyway so I will take the job offer and I will tell my supervisor tomorrow." He remembered what the Bishop had told him. If he stayed in the right relationship with God, blessing would chase him down. Bishop Shepherd's voice broke his concentration, "Okay, Pastor Kelvin. We can finalize the technicalities when you are ready. I am able to also help you get back your driver's license too." "May God bless you, Bishop!" Kelvin shouted louder into the phone than he meant to do. After the Bishop got off the phone, Kelvin got down on his knees beside his bed. He did not want any time to get between his blessing and his thanksgiving. Kelvin began to pray and thank God for answering his prayer. The next day when Kelvin made it to work his supervisor told him that he had received a promotion as a supervisor, he would have his own crew and that he was going to get a raise on his next paycheck.

At first, Kelvin did not know what to say, but as soon as he could muster the words he told his supervisor, "Look, I appreciate the offer, but I came today to give you a week notice about leaving." "What's wrong, Kelvin? Haven't I been good to you since you have been working here?" his supervisor was puzzled. He had been watching how Kelvin worked like a man on a mission. He had been in upper management's ear for weeks saying if they didn't do something, this one was going to leave them. Construction was one of those high turnover jobs where workers would quit because they were injured or because the worker was too hard. Kelvin had adapted very well and had shown great leadership skills. Men naturally followed him with him having the authority to guide them. Kelvin replied, "Yes, you have given me opportunities to learn and for that I am deeply grateful; however, I have Masterful plans with God." That explained everything. The supervisor could better understand why men followed him. Kelvin was a man of God. "Kelvin, I mean, Minister Johnson, if you feel that strongly about it I have no other option, but to grant your request. If the need is that urgent you may leave now if you want, and if you need a referral, it would be my honor to write a letter of recommendation for you. You have been outstanding," his supervisor said with mixed emotions. Kelvin got his pay and shook his supervisor's hand and left.

Kelvin called Bishop Shepherd and told him that he could make it to the church that evening to speak. "Well now, that's great because I really need you. My deacons are not ready to deliver sermons yet and having a true man of God present to usher in the Spirit of the Lord would mean so much to me," Bishop Shepherd said.

Kelvin got on his knees and started to pray. He asked God for strength, knowledge, understanding, and to give him a sermon for tonight. Kelvin got up, began to read and study his Bible. He wanted to be ready for God's people. Later in the evening, he caught the bus to church. The parking lot was packed with cars. Kelvin's nerves tried to get the best of him, but he took in a deep breath and proceeded inside. The deacons greeted him with love and walked Kelvin to his study. Deacon John handed Kelvin some papers and told him that this was what he wrote for Kelvin to speak.

"Thank you, Deacon, but I have my own notes and I really do appreciate your help but I prefer to receive my messages straight from our Holy Father," Kelvin informed him. The choir got up and started to sing '*It Is Me Again, Lord*'. The congregation of members and local visitors of the church were still streaming in. Deacon John went to the podium and instructed everyone to calm down because it was time to be fed the message. It was his job to bring the service to order. He introduced Kelvin and asked everyone to greet him as he approached the microphone. As Kelvin came in everyone stood up and gave him a standing ovation. Kelvin walked to the pulpit and took the microphone. "God is in this building tonight. I can just feel him moving all in this place. Look at how you all just greeted me, not knowing whether I can preach or not," Kelvin joked. Everyone laughed and Kelvin said, "Let us turn our Bibles to the Old Testament. We are going to the book of Job. You know, Job is one of the most faithful men that have ever walked with God. Out of all the things that Satan had put Job through, Job still held his faith. Satan destroyed Job's livestock, his kids, everything he had. Satan even touched his body by putting sores all over him but Job still held on." By the time Kelvin was deep in his message most of the congregation was on their feet. Deacon John hunched Deacon Eley and said "I can see why Bishop talked so good about him, this Kelvin Johnson is awesome. He's preaching the Word, now!" They looked at each other and smiled.

Then Kelvin began to move around and said "With my spiritual eyes, I can see there are a lot of Jobs in here tonight." Kelvin said, "You know we are all sort of like Job. I am quite sure most of us have been through something in our life at one time or another where we felt like God had took His loving hedge away from around us. Be I stopped by here tonight on my way to Heaven to tell you, it might not have been everything we had like Job but we have walked that troublesome path. Before I leave here tonight I am going to give you my testimony you know I been through a storm myself. I sinned against God. I had to make the decision to fight against what Satan offered me to get my sanity back. But, before then, I ate and lived worse than dogs on the streets. I took my eye off God, but as you can see He never took His eyes off of me.

Andre, a former drug addict, jumped up from his seat. He began to witness how the Lord had freed him from the bondage of drugs, a promiscuous life and started praising God. As if on cue, various people throughout the congregation started jumping up and confessing of how the Lord had freed them from their various bondages of a sin filled life. They too began praising God. Then the musicians started playing and then the Spirit of the Lord started moving all around the church and when it fell upon Kelvin. Kelvin began shouting and praising the Lord. He began to dance like David and he was dancing all over the pulpit. Bishop Shepherd walked in just in time to see that his church was in the spirit. Deacon John walked up to him saying, "Bishop, I see why you wanted this Kelvin Johnson fellow!" Bishop Shepherd said, "It is not my doing…it is of God." Bishop ran up on the pulpit and joined in on the shouting himself. After a while, the musician slowed down and the congregation appeared to be calming down. The Spirit had shifted in the church and they had allowed it to move until it was completed. Kelvin acknowledged and publicly thanked the Bishop for the opportunity to speak to his people in his absence. He made room for the Bishop to close out the service. As his final remark, Kelvin said, "We all are going through our storms but it is up to us to fight it and see our way out." Kelvin continued, "Look at me see how God has brought me through and what He has brought me through He can do the same for you."

The Bishop said the doors of the church were now open and asked if there was anyone going through a storm or just want God to turn things around in your life let them come. People were coming up for prayer and the aisles were full. Bishop said, "God is in this building." Bishop Shepherd asked the deacons and prayer team to come up and help the worshippers pray for all that they wanted God to move in their lives.

Once the church service was over and everyone had left and Bishop gave Kelvin the keys to the house. He said, "I told you, my Brother everything was going to be alright." Kelvin was headed to the bus stop overjoyed by the experience he had just witnessed. He felt hopeful and encouraged. He was deep in his thoughts as he was reliving the experience when he heard Bishop's voice. "Hey, Kelvin let's go to the Waffle House to have a bite to eat!" Kelvin opened his eyes to see the Bishop had pulled his Mercedes 350 over in front of him. Kelvin got in the car and they were drove to the Waffle House on Upper Alabama of Decatur. Bishop said "Tomorrow we are going down to the DMV to get your driver's license." After they were ordering their food, the Bishop told Kelvin his next sermon will be in three days. Bishop Shepherd said, "I am not going to ask you are you ready because I know you will be sure to be ready." Bishop Shepherd told Kelvin about a big Baptist convention that is coming up in about two weeks. Bishop Shepherd said, "I would love for you to come with me. These ministers will be coming from all over the United States. Kelvin, they are awesome I know you have probably been before but just think about it because I know you would enjoy it." As they were ordering Kim, the waitress who normally waits on the Bishop and his guests when they dine at the restaurant. She knows most of the Bishop's guest, but there was a new face in the crowd. Kim spoke to the Bishop said, "Bishop, who is this handsome young man you have with you?" Bishop said, "Well, hello, Kim. I am fine today. How are you? He has a mouth ask him." Kim asked Kelvin, "Can you talk or do Bishop have to speak for you?" Kelvin said to Kim, "I assure you, I can talk. What is it you want to ask?" Kim said "Just want to know if are you married?" Kelvin replied, "My wife passed away over twenty years ago." Kim gave her appropriate condolences then she said, "Can I give you my number?" Kelvin said, "Are you sure that would be a good idea? You know, I am a man of God and I don't mess around. I would probably be wasting your time" Kim was persistent, "This is my number. I got to go and wait on my other customers, but call me. I get off at nine tonight." Bishop said, "She is a nice lady, but you just take your time. Kelvin, there is a lot of beautiful single business ladies that are right at your church who are looking for a good God-fearing man like you."

Restoration Comes after Rededication

The next day, Bishop picked up Kelvin to get his driver's license. Bishop gave Kelvin one of his older Mercedes Benzes. Kelvin told Bishop, "Man, I just don't know what to say anymore." Bishop said while handing him the key to the house is on the same ring, as well. This is the address and directions to the house so go get your things from the hotel. Take them to your new home."

Kelvin made it back to the hotel to get his things and put them in the trunk of his car. He stopped by and checked out. Mr. Carl asked him, "Are you leaving town? Kelvin replied, "No, I have been blessed with a new job and a new house." Mr. Carl looked at him suspiciously and said "I hope the best for you, Kelvin. I hate to lose you because you were such a good guest." Kelvin said his goodbyes to the other tenants. He got on the interstate to go to his new house.

A few miles into his journey his phone rung. He picked up and said "Hello." Casandra said "I saw you while ago, but you did not see me. Man, when did you get that nice car?" Kelvin replied, "It was a gift." Casandra said, "Wow! I wish I could receive a gift like that. By the way, where are you going? Kelvin answered her saying, "God has blessed me again with a house. It sounds almost to good to be true, but I think I have finally turned the corner and my season of blessings and restoration has begun." Casandra said, "You have a house?!" To which Kelvin replied, "Yes."

Casandra said, "Look, come around here to get me because I want to check out that house with you." Kelvin turned around to go pick her up. They had not seen each other in a few days so they spend the drive time catching up on the life changes Kelvin had made since their last conversation as they were headed to Stone Mountain, Georgia. Once there, they rode around the neighborhood. Casandra looked wild eyed like a kid in a candy store. She said "You know this is the wealthy "white" section of Stone Mountain. Man, how can you afford this? You really must know somebody." Kelvin chuckled in disbelief as he drove silently to his new address. He pulled up in the driveway. Kelvin said, "Man, this is nice!"

Casandra could not take her eyes off of the house. She said, "What are you doing? Really…tell me what have you got yourself into, Kelvin?" Kelvin said, "This is a gift from the Bishop…the car and the house. Casandra said, "I have been knowing the Bishop for a long time and he never gave me a Mercedes or a big house! All I can get is a ride back and forth to the hotel." She looked at Kelvin and said, "You know you are a blessed man. These gifts are not from the Bishop. They are blessings from God." They went inside the arched doorway. The foyer was huge! The gleaming chandelier hung in the middle of an oval stairwell that split on the second level to run up both sides of the wall. The space very tastefully decorated and it was massive. The imported tiled floors echoed their footsteps as they made their way to the living room. The huge fireplace that was the focal point for the sitting area was so beautiful, as was the wall to wall carpet. The executive styled leather furniture with the mahogany bookcase, which was well polished to perfection, reeked of wealth and status. On the sofa table stood a crystal brandy shifter filled with very expensive cognac and the best crystal goblets money could buy. There was elegance, charm, and detail in every nook and cranny of the room. The scenic pictures that hung on the walls reminded Kelvin of the North Carolina mountains and hills where he grew up. The house was already fully furnished in Kelvin's specific taste, if that could be possible. It was as if he had ordered the house himself.

He turned to go to the next room and was startled by Andre, the butler. Good afternoon, "Pastor Johnson," Andre said. 'Bishop Shepherd asked me to be here to ensure you were made comfortable upon your arrival. I took the liberty of ensuring your favorite items were in place just as you described to him during your conversations. You will find that the Bishop pays very close attention to the details of every single person he meets. It is one of his most endearing traits. He also asked me to collect whatever you brought with you as you won't be needing those things any longer while you are here." Andre continued. "I am taking you on a tour of the house to show you how to get around and how to operate the TV, sound equipment, and the other things. If you have any questions once I leave you, you just press this remote and I will come to you." He handed Kelvin a small remote that fitted right on the loop with his keys to the house and car keys.

Kelvin stood in shock, with his mouth open, looking at Casandra who was also floored. They knew the house would be beautiful inside, but to have a butler was a bit more than either of them could have imagined. Kelvin introduced Casandra to Andre and they walked from room to room and then followed Andre as he went upstairs.

Upstairs were three bedrooms, each with its own suite consisting of bathroom, dressing area and walk-in closet. The master bedroom had a high raised Jacuzzi tub and a stand-alone shower with eight jets of water located at different angles and a rain shower head. It also had a toilet room and two walk-in closets. Kelvin was trying all he could not to jump up and down to show his excitement. The bathroom even had a urinal. Andre joked that the previous owner had it installed to save his marriage, at which they both laughed like it was an inside joke that Casandra was not privy to understand.

When they returned downstairs, Casandra looked through the back dining room window and saw a large oval swimming pool. She excitedly said "Kelvin, look you have a swimming pool out back!" "We will have to take a closer look at that, now won't we?" Kelvin joked at her while walking to the back-patio door.

Just as they were walking around the opposite side of the pool admiring its size they thought they heard someone move in the hedges. When they looked over by the fence, the guy standing there asked if they there to service the pool. Casandra said, "Hey, look here…" but, then Kelvin cut her off, "No, I am actually your new neighbor, Pastor Kelvin Johnson." Mr. Charles Winston Brown turned red, he was so embarrassed for calling them pool staff. He had watched them when they drove up and wanted to be sure they were not there to rob the house. He was a member of the Neighborhood Watch and he was the only one who wasn't too fearful to ask them questions. The other neighbors choose to stand in their windows watching while holding their fingers hovering over 911, just in case things went downhill. He regained him composure and said, "Well, is that right? Welcome to the neighborhood! I am Charlie Brown!" He shook Kelvin's hand uncontrollably until Kelvin physically released his hand from his grip. Kelvin politely introduced Casandra as his house guest. Mr. Charlie told Kelvin that it was a good neighborhood, where everyone minded their own business, but looked out for each other. "You know; you are the first one that ever moved in this neighborhood." Mr. Charlie stated almost whispering. Casandra was getting very upset with the rudeness of this man, she said loudly, "What? Exactly what do you mean by "first one?" Is that your way of saying "black people?" Mr. Charlie turned redder than a beet this time and replied, "Yes, that's what I meant, but I didn't mean to insult you." Kelvin said, "I thank you for the rundown of the neighborhood." and they turned to begin to walking away from the fence. Casandra said "I don't care where you go you are going always run into one of them." Kelvin replied, "Yes, you're right, but they are God's people, too."

The Revisit

Two months past and Kelvin had been doing a marvelous job at the church. The convention that Bishop took him to went very well. Kelvin was finally getting settled in to enjoy his new house and new life. However, where there is good there is also bad. Kelvin worked in his yard all that day. He was exhausted. When night time came he went inside his house to rest. He showered, laid down, and he closed his eyes to fall asleep. He heard a voice call him. It woke him up! Kelvin sat straight up in his bed looking in the direction of the voice. He angrily said "What you are doing in my home?" Kelvin reached for his baseball bat that was beside his bed.

The voice laughingly said "Kelvin you are not going to need that!" Kelvin shouted, "Just get out of my house!" The voice said, "Let me introduce myself, Sir. My name is Barnabas. I come tonight to give you whatever you desire or need." Kelvin said, "Look, I don't need nothing you have to give or nothing you plan on selling." That is when Barnabas pulled out of his jacket a crack pipe with crack already on it. He started to smoke it. He looked at Kelvin as he inhaled the white smoke and blown the residuals out toward Kelvin's face. He handed it to Kelvin and told him to take hit. "There is no one going to know or going to see you smoke it, it will be our little secret," Barnabas whispered.

Barnabas told Kelvin that he could give him whatever the Bishop had. He could make him higher than any Bishop. "Even more money…I can give you your own business and you could have riches upon riches. I'm talking about land as far as you can see." Kelvin said "What I have to do to get all these things you have to offer me." Barnabas said, "First take a hit of this and then we will talk business. Kelvin looked at the crack pipe. He took it in his hand. Barnabas started to smile. As soon as Kelvin spoke "Jesus help me," Kelvin dropped the crack pipe. He looked at Barnabas and said, "I know who you are Satan. You cannot fool me. You think I would go back to your streets and live like a dog for you. You tricked me over twenty years ago but now that I am older stronger and much wiser, you can take your bag of lies somewhere else!" Kelvin stood by the side of his bed and dropped to his folded his hands as if to pray.

"You have no more power over me and my body. Satan, go back where you came from. Satan, get thee behind me in the name of Jesus!" Kelvin declared. Satan once again disappeared from Kelvin. While on his knees Kelvin began to talk, praying to Jesus. Kelvin's words were, "Father, I need you to shield me from my enemy. Father, I keep thinking about the twenty years I stayed out in the street. Father, I don't want to ever live that lifestyle anymore, but Father, the temptation is so hard sometimes I am afraid because I don't want to fail, I am scared. Father what would happen if I did get real, and just take one hit would I go back in the street for another twenty years to live or would I perish and die? Father, I am scared I don't want to go back out there and perish. I want to live for my Lord Jesus Christ I have had my share of ups and downs. Lord, the only thing I want to get high off on is You. Father, I need Your help because by myself, I am weak and I am nothing. Father keep Your arms wrapped around me for my comfort and safety. Father, as I pray to the Father help me fight my demons. Let them crumble at my feet at the sound of Your Name Amen."

Kelvin stood up from his knees, laid down on his bed, and before he knew it was morning. Kelvin s phone rung. When he picked it up, it was the Bishop. Bishop said, "Good morning, Brother!" Kelvin replied, "Good morning Bishop!"

Bishop asked, "Is everything alright?" Kelvin answered, "Yes, all is well. Why do you ask?" The Bishop said "I had a dream last night that one of my sheep's were fighting a wolf. The wolf was trying to get my sheep to leave the herd to follow him off into the wilderness to be eaten alive. The wolf kept telling the sheep about how green the grass was over there in the beyond…on the other side. My sheep was weakening and started taking off behind the wolf. Then my alarm clock awakened me. I could not go back to sleep, but you came to mind. So, I called you to see if everything was alright." Kelvin was humbled. He looked up to God with gratitude. He said "Bishop, your dream was true. You have miraculous insight. You saw the sheep which was me and you saw a wolf who was Satan. Satan tried to get me to leave the church and follow him back out in the wilderness, but I rebuked him in the Name of Jesus." Bishop said. "We all have fallen short to the glory of our Father, my Brother. Our encounters with Satan are real. He tried to attack me as well, and like you, I put that rascal in his place. You know that one thing I can say about Satan is that he is always on his job working to try to get us to follow him to hell, but like I always say the Devil is a liar! If we can believe that one truth, we won't fall prey to his schemes and promises of fulfilling our desires. He dangles those things which are our weakness before us in order to entice us away from our Savior." Continue to stay strong in the power of the Lord and call upon His Name when you need extra strength. He knows and He cares for us. Let's get a few more minutes of shut eye before we get up for this day." Kelvin said, "Amen! That sounds good to me. Thank you Bishop." He hung up the phone and thank God for having Godly people in his life who not only taught him love, but were close enough to feel his pains.

Casandra received a promotion on her job. She was so happy she called the Bishop and asked him to pray for her regarding her new position on her job. She then called Kelvin to inform him. Kelvin told her he was very proud of her. He told her he just knew her blessing was going to come soon. Casandra told Kelvin that she was moving out of the hotel room and into a house with a fence around it. She planned to move in her new home in the next two weeks. She asked Kelvin to help her move. Kelvin said he would if she told him when she had a scheduled date.

Kelvin's sermons for the people were getting stronger and stronger. Kelvin had every seat filled up in the church every Sunday he preached. Bishop told Kelvin that he will have to get a larger church because they will have people all outside just waiting to hear the next sermon and get a good seat. Bishop asked Kelvin to go with him because he wanted his opinion on a property that was for sale. They drove to Downtown Atlanta near the infamous Jackson Street area.

Bishop lead the way to show Kelvin the property. Bishop said, "I want to build right here. I am claiming this property, Kelvin." Kelvin looked and said, "Wow, Bishop! This a lot of property in one of the priciest neighborhoods we could get in." Bishop said, "Yes, it is. God is going to get it for us to build a nice church on it. That is what I believe." Bishop asked "Kelvin, what do you think?" Kelvin answer, "Ask. Believe. Receive." He confirmed that he thought it would be great for the new church. The location was stellar; and although the price was high, it was a worthy investment to put a church in the location to get the spillover from all the tourist and people who came to the district during the year. It would require an extra effort, but Kelvin had seen the Bishop at work so he knew the Bishop was well up to making it happen if it was at all possible.

As they were walking back to the car, Bishop said "Kelvin, I think it is about time you have your own church again." Kelvin said "What do you mean Bishop?" Bishop said, "Kelvin, you have been under my wings long enough. I know it is time for you to pastor your own church. You are standing where I am going to build this new church and I will pastor it. Kelvin said "Bishop, may God bless you." They made it back. Kelvin went home and he got down on his knees and began to praise and thank God for blessing him one more time. Then Kelvin told God thanks for my blessing. And, Father I love what you are doing for me, but what I want most of all is to see my family just one more time before I leave this world. Father, I have a daughter and a son that I would love to see again just one more time, Father." As Kelvin was praying to God the Bishop was on the phone talking to Casandra. Bishop asked her if Pastor Kelvin have any family. Casandra said, "I heard him speak about his children a couple of time or so. I said I would find them one day and invite them to the church to hear their father." Casandra admittedly had got on the computer to do a search for Kelvin Johnson's next of kin several times, but regrettably she found nothing. The Bishop asked her if she would continue to pursue her quest to find Kelvin's family. "It is just not right that his family does not know what the Lord has done in his life," the Bishop reasoned.

A few weeks later, Casandra saw where someone left a message in her inbox saying he knew a Kelvin Johnson but he had not seen or heard from him in almost twenty years or more. When Casandra emailed them back, she asked the age of the Kelvin Johnson he knew and if he would describe him. In his reply he told Kelvin's right age, he had his height right, and he showed a picture of what could have been what Kelvin looked like when he was younger. Casandra email him back and asked what relation was he to the person he knew. Alvin said, "My name is Alvin Johnson. Kelvin Johnson is my only living brother and I am his only living brother, as well."

Casandra was so excited! She had found Kelvin's family! Her hands were shaking as she emailed him her telephone number and asked him to call her. Alvin got off the computer immediately and called Casandra, Casandra asked Alvin when was the last time he had seen his brother. Alvin said it has been over twenty years and then Alvin paused. "Why are you getting in touch with me? Is he okay? He is not dead is he?" "Wow, Chief," Casandra said, "No, he is not dead, sick, disabled, or anything negative like that. He is doing quite well." Alvin gave a sigh of relief. "Well, that is music to my ears. It is good to hear he is doing okay. I remember the last time saw Kelvin he was doing really bad. He did not want anyone to help him. My brother had a lot of pride. He did not want anyone to feel pity for him. He just would not let any of us help him nor would he go for professional help. He just wanted to stay out on the streets and get high all the time. But if you had met him before he got on that mess you would have loved him too. He has always been a warm loving and caring person to everyone." Alvin rambled.

Casandra said, "You are right and your brother is here in Atlanta. He was still on the streets but God picked him up and turned him around." Alvin was overjoyed to hear that his prayers for his brother had been answered. "I have been praying for my brother to find peace and restoration, Casandra. I have fasted and prayed to God for my brother and for his children. It is not that I don't believe you Casandra. I need to know that what you say is true. Casandra said, "Yes, it is all true." Alvin said it again, "Wow! God really did answer my prayer." Casandra asked, "Where are his kids who he always talk about." Alvin said, "They are still here in Chattanooga, Tennessee with me. They are doing very well. They always talk about when will they ever see their daddy again, especially his daughter." Alvin said, "Hold up, I am going to call her right now on three-way." Casandra said "Okay." Alvin called his niece Dericka, first. When Dericka picked up the phone she said, 'Uncle Alvin, how are you doing today? Alvin said, "I am okay." then Dericka said. "Uncle Alvin, I've been meaning to call you to tell you I had this crazy dream last night. I was standing in this familiar place and when I looked I saw this man. He was smiling at me and as I was walking closer he kept smiling. When I got closer I could see that he was my daddy. He was looking real handsome, so neat and clean. Alvin said, "Well, what I am going to tell you is going to shock you." Dericka said, "Uncle Alvin" Please do not tell me that my daddy is dead! I could not take that right now, especially after last night's dream." Alvin quickly quieted her "No, child, he is not dead, but I can tell you this, your dreams are good because I have you on a three way call with a lady name Casandra. She told me that your daddy is off the streets. And…just like you dreamed…he is doing very well for himself."

Dericka started to cry and Alvin said, 'Why are you crying?" Casandra said "Let that child in me cry because she is happy and her daddy is free from them demon spirits that took a hold on him for all those years," Dericka started doing her holy dance, Casandra said what is that sound Alvin said she is probably doing her Holy Dance on the phone.

Casandra started laughing and said "Praise the Lord." After Dericka finished. Casandra said "He is going to preach for the first time as pastor at our church Sunday. Your daddy is on fire when it comes down to preaching. He has been with us for a while but know my Bishop has given him the church and I would like for you all to come down and support him." Dericka said, "You tell my daddy Kelvin Jr. and I are going to be there when he

preaches." Casandra said, "I am not going to tell him I want you to surprise him." Dericka was happy and excited she said, "Okay, sure will. I cannot wait to see daddy." Casandra said, "He talks about his kids all the time. By the way, do you know how to get in touch with all your other relatives. It would really surprise him if all of his siblings could be there.

Dericka did what she does every day she cooked and packed some food in a bag and she got in her car and drove to Third and North Streets. She got out of her car, walked around. She looked for Nine, a local junkie that frequented the area. Dericka asked Nine if he had seen her brother. Nine said, "You know he is back there doing his thing. Nine asked Dericka, "When are you going let me take you to dinner?" Dericka tried very politely to tell him, "Never!" Nine said, "That is what they all say, but you'll be back. You just wait and see." Dericka replied, "Okay. Goodbye, Nine." She walked over to the abandon building where she thought she had seen Kelvin Jr. Kelvin Jr. saw Dericka coming and tried to hide his crack pipe. This was his way of both respecting his sister and being ashamed of his condition.

Dericka said, "Kelvin, Jr., I saw you and I saw you were trying to hide your drugs, but you cannot hide it from God! I still pray for you. I pray every day and every night that you will be delivered from this sickness." Dericka said, "Here is your lunch. Enjoy it. It is beef stew from last night when you did not come home to eat. I also wanted to give you some good news." Kelvin Jr. said, "And what may that be?" Dericka said, "Uncle Alvin has located our daddy." Kelvin Jr. said, "I know you are not fooling around with drugs are you?" Dericka said, "No, Kelvin, really! He had been talking with this lady named Casandra and they called me on three-way. She told me that our daddy was still alive and he is doing quite well for himself now. Our dad was a survivor, Kelvin, Jr.!"

Kelvin Jr. did not know what to say or think. This news confused him. He was small when their father left so he had always thought of him as a weakling who gave in to the drugs. Could this be true? Dericka told Kelvin about the family's plan to go see Kelvin preach his first sermon at the church where he was the pastor, in Atlanta. It was to be a big surprise. Kelvin, Jr. asked, "What is daddy doing in Atlanta?" Dericka said, "I told you, silly! He is back preaching again and he has his own church." Kelvin Jr. said, "Well, tell him I said hello." Dericka said, "You are not coming?" Kelvin Jr. quickly replied, "No! "I am not going to see my daddy looking like this." Dericka said, "Look out of all the people in the world you would not think your daddy would not understand because you are his seed and this did happen to you for you to be ashamed, but it happened to you to make you a living testimony, one day you are going to be able to tell someone what you went through and how you overcame it. That is why I've always come to see about you because I know that God is going to see you through this journey. Kelvin, Jr. I pray day and every night for you to leave these streets alone. I pray that God deliver you from this demon. Don't you see, God did it for your daddy. So I know He can do the same for you." Dericka said "Kelvin Jr., I need for you to get yourself together because we are going to Atlanta to see our daddy." Then one of Kelvin Jr. friends walked over and said, "Hey, KJ, have you finished with my pipe yet?" Dericka looked at Kelvin, Jr. and said, "Come on back home Kelvin Jr. Leave these streets to the streets."

The Bishop caught up with Casandra one Sunday morning as she was walking into the vestibule. He asked her the status of finding some of Kelvin's people. Casandra replied, "Yes. As a matter of fact, I found his brother and his daughter. Bishop said, "Well, are they coming to see Kelvin on his Day of Rejoicing?" Casandra said, "They would not miss it for the world."

Time passed and it was the Sunday morning of Kelvin's Day of Rejoicing. Everyone was coming to the church house. The cars were parking everywhere. Kelvin was in the back in the preacher study praying to ask God to give him a wonderful sermon for today. In the church the deacon said a couple of words and then he turned it over to the choir. The choir got up and began to sing *"Victory Is Mine."* Everyone stood up, singing, clapping their hands, and praising the Lord. Kelvin walked out of the back and sat in the pulpit. From a distance, Dericka could see her father. She just could not hold back the tears. She began to cry a river of tears from all the times she missed the man she saw standing before the people. She was crying because she missed him so much. Alvin gave her some tissue to wipe her eyes. The choir stopped singing and the deacon turned the services over to the pastor. Kelvin grabbed the microphone and started singing *"I Have Been In The Storm."* Today, Kelvin was singing like he had never sung before. This time Dericka stood up with everyone else to praise God. When Kelvin finished, he told the church that the message for today is going to be parents. It is entitled, *"Don't Leave Your Little Children."*

"You know God gave us these beautiful kids. He gave them to us for a reason and sometimes we just don't know how precious they are until they are taken away. You know I am a witness to that because I had a beautiful family before. I lost everything, even those precious children God left in my care. I was so careless with the gifts God had given me. He placed them in my care and I forgot I was on duty. I needed so much forgiveness to get me out of the mess I put myself in. Now, I have had to pray and ask him to help me find what I lost. Today if any of you that have children here with you, I want you to tell them how much you love them and how much you appreciate them. Give them a big hug and a kiss. Then turn to your neighbor and say "God is going to bless you and your children abundantly and as I speak it into existence, there shall be no weapon formed against, you and yours. Amen." Then Kelvin began to weep and tell the church how he abandoned his kids and how the social service people just took them away. He stated that it is because of his actions that he may never see them again. Then he paused for a minute and he told the church he apologized for his action and for crying instead of giving them the message. Kelvin sat down. and his assistance finished the sermon and then Deacon John got up and he asked did anyone want to be saved today or just want prayer so the people was coming up. Kelvin got up and started praying for the people. Kelvin finished praying and Casandra walked up and told Kelvin she had some people who wanted to see him after church. Kelvin finished praying.

Casandra grabbed Kelvin by the hand and said, "Follow me," Kelvin said, "You know I cannot be long because I need to see the Bishop." Casandra said, "Okay, but as of now, the Bishop will just have to wait." Kelvin said "I hope this is important" They made it to the back of the church. Kelvin said, 'Who it is anyway." Casandra said, "Look across the room." Kelvin said, "You know my vision is getting dim."

Kevin squinted his eyes as he walked closer, then he stopped in his tracks and said, "Oh my Lord…That is Alvin…my brother!" Alvin ran over and gave Kelvin a huge hug. Alvin and Kelvin were both crying. Kelvin said, "Brother, I have not seen you in over twenty some odd years. Alvin said, "Look who I brought with me..." as he stepped aside. Dericka couldn't wait any longer she ran over and hugged her father's neck.

Kelvin said, "I knew exactly who you were Dericka. You look identical to your mother. You have grown up to be a beautiful young lady." The rest of Kelvin's family came to greet him. Kelvin had to sit down to take it all in. Another prayer answered. He was having the time of his life. Kelvin and Dericka began to walk off to talk. Kelvin asked, "How is my son? How is Kelvin, Jr.? Tell him that I love him God is going to take that demon away from him because he is favored by God. Dericka said, "Daddy, how did you know?" Kelvin said, "I seen him in my dreams I saw how he was being chased by those same demons that had me. He was running and looking for protection. What he does not know is that God is not going to let anyone or anything harm one hair on his head. God has been with him all the time and God has carried him through the darkness but now it is time for him to come to the light." Dericka was still holding her daddy's hand. She was telling him how much she missed him and how happy she is at this moment. She said "Daddy, I just cannot stop smiling. I feel just like I am a little girl again." Kelvin said, "It is okay. You are going to always be my little girl. It's okay."

Kelvin invited everyone to his home and when they saw it they could not believe their eyes Alvin said, "Lord have mercy! Man, this is a beautiful home!" Kelvin said, "Thank you Alvin." Dericka said, "Dad, you really got it going on in Atlanta, huh?" Kelvin said, "God has blessed me with this nice home. He has blessed me to see my family again." Kelvin continued, 'Man, it is hard to believe that you are actually here! Would someone pinch me and woke me up?" Then, just as quickly he said, "Don't pinch me! If this is a dream let me just keep on dreaming!" Everyone just laughed. Kelvin asked if anyone was hungry. Everyone said in unison, "Yes!" Casandra said, "I can cook some chicken, if that is what everyone wants to eat." While she was cooking the brothers were telling stories about the old day and how they struggled with a family of nine. Casandra asked, "There were nine of you all? Alvin answered, "Yes, but over the years some of us began to die off. I really miss my family members who have left us here."

Kelvin said, "Yes, I miss them too and may God bless them where they are sleeping." Then he showed Dericka her room in his home. Dericka walked in it and she said, "Dad, you must have known this day would have come to pass." Kelvin said, "I always kept my faith and believe that I would see my babies again someday. That is why I prepared this room for you with your favorite colors on the bed. "You remembered, Daddy!" Dericka said, "You are right and purple is still my favorite color." Then she saw the old rag doll sitting in the upper corner of her headboard. Tears filled her eyes as she softly said, "Dad, I know this is not that old doll I use to drag around. How is it that you have kept it all these years?" Kelvin said, "I kept it in my back sack wrapped up in plastic." Kelvin said, "Baby, I have to get up early tomorrow morning. I better be getting some sleep, okay."

The next morning, they sat and reminisced how life was when things was much simpler. They ate breakfast and they were about to say their goodbyes when Kelvin said "Hold up! I am going to follow you all back to Chattanooga." Alvin said, "Okay…well let's go!" They made it back to Chattanooga, Tennessee just before sunset. Kelvin rode around the old neighborhood with Dericka with him.

Later as they drove up to the driveway to Dericka's house Kelvin asked, "Do you think he is here?" Dericka pursed her bottom lip, because she did not want to be the one tattling on her brother, but she was not going to cover up for him neither. She said, "No, he enjoys hanging out on the streets. He hardly comes here unless he is hungry. When he does, I feed him." Kelvin said, "That is very good of you, but you can't let him disrespect you, not for any reason because he is filled with his own demons." Dericka showed her father where Kelvin Jr. usually hung out. When Kelvin could see his son from afar it made his heart break in several small pieces. He had seen this look before. The faces of the hundreds of mothers with their sons who wanted to straighten their lives flashed before him. Kelvin never dreamed that his own son would ever be in the state of those young men.

He asked Dericka to wait in the car as he walked over to Kelvin Jr. to say hello to his son. Kelvin Jr. looked up at him like he was trying to remember where he knew him from. Kelvin hugged him and said, "Son, God is going to deliver you whenever you get tired of this world. God allows you to choose when you have had enough. He is not going to make you choose until you are ready. You must do that on your own, but come here because I want you to know I am not here to give you a lecture. I am here to tell you that I love you. I am sorry for the things I let you and your sister go through. I cannot take them back, but I wish I could. If and when you decide to go to rehab you are welcomed to come to Atlanta. If you choose to stay here and if you ever need me, call me. Dericka will always know how to reach me. Son, I love you." Kelvin Jr. gave his dad another hug. He did not want to let go.

As they stood there in a solid embrace, Dericka walked over. Very softly, she asked, "Can we pray together as a family like we used to do when Mom was alive? Together, the three of them stood in the middle of the courtyard crying and praying. When it came time to let go, Kelvin hugged and kissed them both. It was after Kelvin had dropped Dericka back at her house and left that he was riding down the interstate. Suddenly, he felt the water as it quietly and warmly traced down his face…he was crying for his son. He was crying for Anna, for Emma, for Andrew and even for Tim. These hot tears fell hot as they soaked the front of his shirt. They were even for him as the people he loved most in the world became a part of the distant scenery that shrunk to almost nothing in his rearview mirror, as he headed to his future.

The End

Made in the USA
Columbia, SC
27 February 2023